CW01085339

Best wishes

Richard and Diana

Colin

10.12

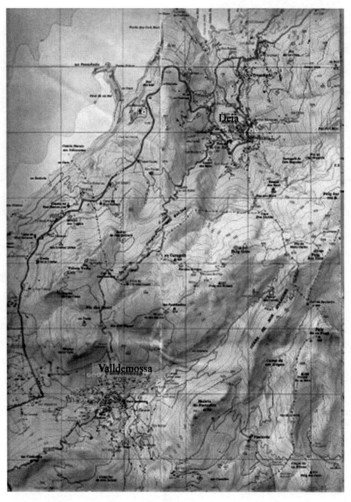

Front cover
Artist: Conrad Sevens, Deia 2005

Journey to Majorca

by

Glyn Pitchford

Grosvenor House
Publishing Limited

All rights reserved
Copyright © Glyn Pitchford, 2012

Glyn Pitchford is hereby identified as author of this
work in accordance with Section 77 of the Copyright, Designs
and Patents Act 1988

The book cover picture is copyright to Glyn Pitchford

This book is published by
Grosvenor House Publishing Ltd
28-30 High Street, Guildford, Surrey, GU1 3EL.
www.grosvenorhousepublishing.co.uk

This book is sold subject to the conditions that it shall not, by way of
trade or otherwise, be lent, resold, hired out or otherwise circulated
without the author's or publisher's prior consent in any form of binding or
cover other than that in which it is published and
without a similar condition including this condition being imposed
on the subsequent purchaser.

A CIP record for this book
is available from the British Library

ISBN 978-1-78148-501-9

www.glynpitchford.co.uk

Dedication

*To Maggie and our two
grandchildren Jack and Freya.*

Acknowledgements

To Jordi, Miguel and Bernardo for their inspiration; Hamish MacGibbon, Richard Jaffa, John Duckers and John Hipkiss for their wise counsel; Avtar for the loan of his secretary, Emma. Also thanks, albeit unwittingly, to Polita, Rafael, Jose-Luis and Sandra, Pepin, Terry L. and Gil, Alister B., tennis coaches Shayne (Majorca) and Matt (Solihull), Pedro, Mike and Jenny, Mike and Bojana, Nick and Deena and their 3 grandchildren; Ron and Barbara, Jane F., Simon and Becky, Chris and Alison, Andy and Gilly, Richard H., Anthony C., Rod A., Mont, cousin Roy, Peter S., Chris Spedding and Griff Rhys Jones.

"Every Journey"

Every journey begins with a small step.
Every race has a starting line.
Keep on reaching out for your goal,
don't give up, just give it time.

When the mountain seems too steep to climb
Just keep moving on, just keep moving on.

When the pathway seems too hard to find
Just keep moving on, just keep moving on.

When the river seems too wide to swim,
Just keep moving on, just keep moving on.

When the battle seems too tough to win,
Just remember this, we must stay strong.

Every journey begins with a small step.
Every race has a starting line.
Keep on reaching out for your goal,
Don't give up, just give it time.
Don't give up, just give it time."

Composed by Sha Armstrong, ©Out of the Ark Ltd
Reproduced with permission and thanks to St.Alphege Infant
School, Solihull

Contents:

Introduction

This account describes a journey. Not just in the physical sense of going from one place to another which it does, but also metaphorically.

In life we are often confronted with canyons to cross. These can seem like insurmountable chasms or unclimbable mountains. We can endure much but need luck and dedication, essential ingredients if we are to achieve our goals.

From humble beginnings my unhappy, sickly childhood was to move into a relatively comfortable adulthood thanks to the support of my parents, my wife and my own determination to succeed.

A kind of metamorphosis took place over time which by chance transported me into another life, a far cry from my early childhood days in Sheffield. And that of my burgeoning professional life in Birmingham. Arguably this story is about two lives. Not only does it contrast these two periods in my own life, but it dwells on some incredible experiences I enjoy when I am on the Mediterranean island of Majorca compared with my life back here in England. I also contrast my own life with that of a Spaniard my wife and I employ at our Majorcan home in the *Serra de Tramuntana,* the mountain range which is located on the northern side of the island.

When on the island the contrast is so vivid, the adventures so improbable, a far cry from that experienced by most tourists.

I describe the local colourful characters I meet and attempt to give a sense of place.

Again for context I highlight some of the local villages and towns, particularly near us such as Valldemossa and Deià, but especially some history, their customs, heritage and food.

Only after moving from Puerto Pollensa, with its largely English bias, to the mountains near Valldemossa, did I truly discover the hidden Majorca and the many different culinary specialities peculiar to this island. Certainly there are too many to mention here and I apologise now for my omissions.

As with Spanish wine and arguably only two decades ago, Spain unquestionably would not have been considered for its quality of food; the actual produce grown in the country, certainly, but not in gastronomic terms. How such times have changed. I have tried to portray some aspects of this in the following pages.

Each year I experience even more quality restaurants on this attractive island, invariably introduced by Spanish friends, largely away from the usual tourist trail.

I am left in no doubt at all that Spain has itself undergone a startling and rapid metamorphosis to arguably becoming one of the top destinations in the world for gastronomy.

Today, in my view, it is up there with France.

These days we spend much time here, particularly in the summer, with our two young grandchildren, Jack and Freya. We regard such time spent with them as incredibly fortunate and invaluable. Invaluable because these two children have enriched our lives and succeeded in bringing home to us the value of simple things. The sheer joy I for one experience when walking with them in the mountains directly accessed from our front door, intent on stalking the wild mountain goats that exist here in vast quantity.

It quickly became apparent once we had moved into this region that I would need a better command of the Spanish language. In the main, the vast majority of the indigenous population around here but especially in Valldemossa do not speak English. So I decided to make an effort. Not a straightforward task, bearing in mind both my age and the sobering fact that the local Majorcan dialect is derived from the Catalan language widely spoken in Catalonia, a northern Spanish province centred around Barcelona. Castilian Spanish would be their second language and English may not be on their radar. Happily and thanks to my connections with Aston University in Birmingham I have become reasonable, though not necessarily fluent, in Spanish. I'm still working on this!

Some pastimes are important to maintain through life, in my case tennis and skiing, together with my voluntary work particularly with the Birmingham Civic Society. All this activity helps to keep me fit in body and mind, the latter some would say being arguable!

I delve only briefly into some aspect of my current professional life as a chartered surveyor centred on Birmingham and Solihull in the West Midlands. Again this is to emphasize context.

Hopefully I demonstrate the rewards which flow from stepping outside of one's comfort zone.

One day I suppose I shall be too old for all this excitement but hopefully not for a good many years yet. At least I shall be left with some lasting and evocative memories of my journey through life.

Chapter 1 Miguel

Puffing a 6" Monte Cristo balancing precariously from his lips, Miguel arrived, carrying a dirty plastic supermarket bag from which he pulled out an octopus which he'd caught that morning. Miguel and Havana cigars are pretty much inseparable. Certainly I have never seen him without one, ash-burned holes in his working trousers giving evidence to this.

He seemed oblivious to his unkempt appearance, his chin wearing the previous day's stubble, his thinning hair greased back. A gaunt, avuncular Majorcan completely at one with the world.

It was late October and I had been invited along with Miguel to take *desayuno,* breakfast, at Jordi's house in the grounds of a typical Spanish hacienda he looks after. The Majorcan sun was struggling to rise over the Tramuntana mountains in the north-west of the island. It looked like the onset of yet another late summer's day, just before the climate was to cool rapidly, yet this was meant to be their autumn.

Earlier that morning, following the previous evening's showers, our host had gone foraging for *setas,* wild mushrooms, and had gathered a few of the 47 or so varieties of herbs growing in the adjoining forest, dense with holm oak and pine trees growing steeply up the partly terraced mountainside.

Soon Miguel had taken over the kitchen, throwing olive oil and roughly chopped garlic into a frying pan. He flicked open his *trinxet*, a largish pocket knife with a bill-hook shaped blade, and deftly sliced up the *pulpo*, the octopus, adding freshly picked mushrooms, some reasonable local red wine and a few of the unpronounceable herbs into the mix. By now my taste buds were coming alive. The aromas danced with the anticipated promise of a new day. I was looking forward to my breakfast.

Meanwhile Jordi had put out a bowl of this year's vintage of mixed bitter strong tasting black and green olives gathered from his ample grounds onto the plastic covered table on the sea-facing terrace adjoining the kitchen. A *barra*, their term for a baguette, came out along with a bowl of the finest eating oranges in the entire world. These were grown in his father-in-law's orchard, down the mountain in Soller. Oranges grown here are a meal in themselves, large, sweet and best of all without pips!

I'd brought a *vino tinto*, a *crianza*-aged red wine from Navarra, and we tucked into breakfast. It seemed the custom to bring one's own '*trinxet*', in my case my swiss army knife.

To finish, I was offered an expresso in a glass, which burned my fingers, followed by a tot of Bell's whisky. Luckily I needed only to drive the 1km back to my house.

I simply had to safely negotiate a narrow winding road which had a 1000ft sheer drop over on my left!

Miguel was a retired *funcionario*, a public servant, having previously been the captain of a fishing ketch for 45 years, operating out of the Port of Soller. The sea beyond Jordi's *casita* was cobalt blue and tranquil. A perfect morning, enabling Miguel to have risen at his usual hour of 3.30am when going fishing, to bring in his catch for our table. As a *pescadora*, a fisherman, his experience in finding whatever catch he thinks is available is second to none, particularly in the bay of Valldemossa upon which we looked out, some way below us.

Out of deference to their English guest, the chat over our food was in Castilian Spanish, not, thankfully, in Majorcan, a language which, I think, belongs to another planet. I can cope with Spanish, although not the dialect coming from Miguel's toothless mouth. Thus I rely on Jordi who, himself, speaks only in broad, clipped Spanish, often mixing his sentences in both Castilian and Majorcan, to translate into marginally more understandable Spanish, giving me half a chance at least of following the banter.

Now his wife, Polita, who looks after their grandchildren every day in Soller whilst their parents are out working, speaks pretty distinctive Spanish. No English, but thankfully her Spanish is clearly understood. When I first met her I mistakenly called her 'Pollita' which means 'small chicken,' which she patently obviously is not. This amused Jordi greatly, putting me right on the correct pronunciation.

I often wished she could join us on these occasions, for my benefit, notwithstanding that this rural society is still surprisingly very much male dominated. This is much to the relief of my non Spanish-speaking wife, Maggie, who appreciates these moments of tranquillity whilst I'm out working on the language.

Well now, Jordi fancies himself as a practical joker. Before I knew better, I asked him how old Miguel was.

"Ah, el Viejo!" he exclaimed, *el Viejo* being his rather fond term for an old man. Others perhaps would have preferred the less derogatory term, *anciano,* the ancient one.

"He is nearly 90 years old".

Well, I thought he looked much younger, and I said as much to Miguel, congratulating him on his wearing well in this his 90th year.

"But senor," he said, looking somewhat doleful, "I am only 74!"

Howls of laughter from Jordi. I realised my having been duped, looking daggers at Jordi who by this time was having trouble hiding his broad grin.

A couple of months passed by before I was to return to the island.

On seeing Jordi I asked how Miguel was.

"Ah, Senor Picfor, he is very poorly, having just had an operation on his "cojones", his privates, and had just come out of hospital."

Well, suspecting this could be yet another practical joke, I told Jordi I was having none of it and that I simply didn't believe him. He became excitable and told me sadly it was true. I thought the worst. It sounded like testicular cancer. So I quietly commiserated and told Jordi to let Miguel know how sorry I was.

When the next day we found ourselves at our usual bar in Valldemossa, I enquired from a relative of Miquel just how he was. I was thanked for asking and told he had fully recovered.

That sounded strange. "Fully recovered?" I asked.

"Yes," came the quick response, "the hernia operation was quite straightforward."

Just occasionally I get to go to the village at about 8am to buy the bread without Jordi. This is because he is needed down in Soller to help his son Pedro slaughter a few sheep or cut into firewood some recently fallen pine trees. Sheer heaven, for me, that is. Everyone I meet in the bar asks me where Jordi is. They know I'm his taxi driver and coffee buyer! Did I mention he never learned to drive a car? He has a scooter and relies on his wife to drive him further afield when I'm not on the island.

"*Muy tranquilo*" they each say to me. "Very quiet", meaning how calm it is without Jordi being about. They are only joking, of course. Well, I think they are!

This in turn means I can have a *café americano*, light up a cheroot at a table outside and quietly read the "*Diario de Mallorca*" or the "*Ultima Hora*", the local newspapers, without interruption.

Unless Miguel is about that is!

If he is, and I am without my travelling translator Jordi, I usually sit with him and steer him onto a subject I already know his views about, so that I can at least appear to be picking up his dialect. That time in the morning he would be sat outside quietly on his own, smoking his Monte Cristo and sipping his *café solo,* the dregs to be diluted with a few drams of Bell's from his personal bottle on the bar table which he always offers to share with me, tipping some into my *americano*.

His family runs this particular bar. It can be quite incestuous in these parts!

His charming wife would be going about her daily shopping, stopping to pass the time of day chatting in her first language, Majorcan, to all the ladies she meets along her route, each pursuing their own quest. At some stage the *senora* would remember to collect Miguel before returning home. In all the years I have been coming to Valldemossa I have not once noted them taking coffee together. It just isn't their custom.

On one such occasion I enquired about how life was in Valldemossa during the Franco dictatorship. He would pause to observe yet another *latino* passing by, a Latin American immigrant, a great many now having settled on the island.

His reply was perhaps surprising, certainly informative:

"Life was better," he said, "under Franco, particularly on this island. Drugs were not a problem, people were more respectful and thieving was not as prevalent as it is today because the penalties were much harsher. Living within the European Union is costly; bring back the peseta."

Most of the people I chat with around these parts say much the same.

Every time we speak in monetary terms, such as with reference to the price of housing, Miguel talks quite excitedly, as with Jordi always quoting in pesetas and making the point that the islanders were much richer under Franco than they are today. On that score I have to quietly disagree with Miguel. Even today many businesses here do appear to be making a decent living out of tourism, notwithstanding the reported high unemployment level.

During the day Valldemossa is heaving and certainly the patisseries and bars are full to the brim, as indeed are the restaurants.

Admittedly the place quietens well before nightfall, the throngs having dissipated, many back to their cruise ships anchored in the bay of Palma, leaving the locals in peace to enjoy the setting sun.

Chapter 2 Jordi

Jordi was born 65 years ago in Jerez in Andalucia on what the Majorcans call the peninsular, the Spanish mainland. His father died when he was only a month old. He never went to school, he told me once. His mother re-married and Jordi was required to work in the fields from the age of 6. At 12 years old he was sent to Majorca, living in Soller nestled in the Tramuntana mountains where he worked in a bakery. Incredibly he worked there until aged 20, slaving from midnight until noon, seven days a week.

He was then to spend two years conscripted into the Spanish navy, serving as a chef aboard a minesweeper. A spell as a builder's labourer followed until eventually he settled as a security guard, residing in his *casita*, a small bungalow, adjoining the *hacienda* within his care, aided by a couple of mean looking German Shepherds.

He was destined to meet his sweetheart when he was 16 and they became a couple after he left the Navy.

Surprisingly perhaps, he really still enjoys cooking, with a figure which goes with the territory. Not for him an ascetic diet. Interestingly though, he neither smokes nor drinks alcohol. His meat pies called, locally, *empanadas*, which are a speciality of the island, are to die for. The best in the region. They are generally packed with pork, sometimes lamb or with peas as a vegetarian alternative. When I'm here for any length of time he makes me 2 or 3 dozen which go in the freezer ready for cooking on demand.

Moreover, his reputation for cooking one of this island's most famous specialities, roast suckling pig, is legendary.

As with most tasks he confronts, he takes his cooking seriously and with pride.

I recall the occasion when my younger son Simon was staying with us along with Becky and the grandchildren. The at times avuncular Jordi asked us to an early dinner. We were impressed when large plates of *fritas mallorquin*, a delicious local speciality of minced meat and small potato cubes fried with garlic in olive oil, were placed in front of us. We all ate with gusto.

Incredibly and to our great surprise out then came a large dish of slow roasted *cabra salvaje*, wild goat, with *ensalada mixta*, mixed salad. The unfortunate beast had strayed onto his land to munch his fruit bushes only to be shot and promptly despatched into his freezer in readiness for serving at a suitable occasion. This was the suitable occasion!

None of us had any idea that a second main course was to be served. Jordi does not tend to do things by halves, or at least when he is in the kitchen. But then neither does Polita.

The grandkids thought they were eating lamb. To eat freshly cooked mountain goat is not something the English are accustomed to. I didn't want to trigger a psychological trauma, so I kept quiet.

Jordi also has a passion for birds, both those in the wild and those he keeps as pets such as canaries of which he has numerous on his terrace. He is a connoisseur. But he likes nonetheless certain birds such as *tordo,* thrush, in his *paella*. Majorcans are partial to eating *tordo,* I suppose as an alternative to rabbit. I am not at all happy eating this poor bird so I always decline notwithstanding that Jordi claims I ate one of Polita's paella which contained thrush, he says, which I ate with relish. I'm not so sure.

I do know however that there is a keen market for exchanging birds between the locals in these mountains.

On Sundays and fiesta days he and Polita regularly entertain their family from Soller and Santa Maria, serving often as many as 20 or 30 of them with a feast, much of which is sourced from their land or in any event home made. It also helps, of course, to be knowledgeable, as Jordi is, about the many varieties of wild mountain herbs growing all around us.

June 2011 was the occasion of a really special *fiesta*, or party. It was Jordi's 65th birthday and he had booked a friend's restaurant out at Montuiri, on the plains heading towards Manacor, home of Rafael Nadal the tennis star. A fascinating small Majorcan *pueblo* totally unspoilt by tourism. Jordi's family from both Majorca and

Barcelona had been invited. All 68 of them. And me. I was privileged to be the only outsider to this celebration. My wife had not yet joined me on the island. As I knew that most could not speak English I thought that this would really test my knowledge of the language.

In fact I only landed at Palma airport at 12 noon on the day of his birthday to be told by mobile phone on arrival that Jordi and Polita would meet me in the town of Palma at 12.30pm and lead me in my hired car to the venue. I had been at Birmingham airport early that morning so I knew I might be a little tired by the time I arrived and it was already a scorching hot day. Happily the plane landed on time and our arrangements worked perfectly.

The occasion was helped by the presence of Rafael, Jordi's brother recently arrived from Barcelona along with his younger daughter, both of whom had a reasonable command of English. When seated, out came plates of *caracoles*, snails, which at first I declined having previously had a really bad experience eating these some years ago in France. But Rafael persuaded me that these were the best, freshly gathered from a snail farm on the island and were rather succulent having been cooked in olive oil and garlic with local herbs. He was absolutely right and I found I couldn't stop eating them. That is, until other courses came out including *pa amb oli, jamon, chorizo,* speciality *tapas* which I describe later and Majorcan olives which were young and very strong. These in my view are an acquired taste. *Arroz con mariscos*, watery rice with seafood, was the main course, not to be confused with *paella* which is very different.

All this was served with *vino tinto del verano*, a summer red wine, meaning we were adding cold soda water to a glass of wine which is a truly refreshing way to drink wine in the heat of the summer.

Rather reminiscent of the Godfather, Jordi then received presents one by one following the banquet. He surprisingly supports Real Madrid and I lost count of the number of the Club's regalia and other souvenirs he was given including a Real Madrid wristlet watch. Alas, not for Jordi the detritus of this modern world we call computers. If only he would accept the inevitable of allowing a PC into his home I for one would find communication with him from over 1000 miles away so much easier.

At least he has a mobile phone, but then who doesn't these days? Unfortunately he does not do texts. If I send him one he will ignore it completely. Either he can't read or, more likely, he hasn't yet admitted to needing spectacles, unlike most people his age!

Afterwards came the speech. I have never seen Jordi lost for words. In fact I would describe him as being garrulous in character, using scores of words when just a handful would do. But on this occasion he stood up to his full height of 5 foot 4 inches and merely exclaimed "Gracias", thank you, and promptly sat down.

I then recall doing a jig with his mother, a lovely lady, which seemingly entertained the multitude and which I gather was captured on video, before beating my retreat up to Valldemossa, leaving the partygoers to their merriment which I heard afterwards lasted well into the night.

Jordi is loyal to the bone. I was introduced to him in 2003 at the time we were buying our *finca*, or country house, though mercifully without too much land, up in the mountains midway between Valldemossa and Deià. We needed to employ a pool maintenance man, doubling up as a security guard for when we were not in residence.

I agreed an appropriate salary which I would pay Jordi for services rendered monthly, as advised by my good friend Pedro, an Estate Agent based in the island's capital, Palma. Pedro happens to be one of those Majorcans with whom most foreigners would take to instantly. He has an endless repertoire of jokes which he tells in impeccable English. When I enquired where *he* takes his holidays he responded as quick as a flash:

"Senor Glyn, but everyday is a holiday here in Palma. My office in the Paseo Maritimo looks out onto the busy marina and the aquamarine sea beyond, the sun keeps shining and I have no desire to leave the island."

The fact that the government gives them a 50% subsidy for both ferry and air travel between the Spanish islands and their mainland seemingly cuts no ice. The islanders are happier staying put.

Jordi also takes his job seriously. Sometimes alarmingly so.

One day I was working in my office at our West Midlands home in Solihull when the phone rang. It was a very excitable Jordi. Eventually my ears tuned into his less than perfect Spanish. It transpired that he had come up to our *finca* to attend to the swimming pool and imagine his shock, he was blurting to me when, to his eternal surprise, he saw that the pool was being used by an ageing man, stark naked.

Clearly the uninvited guest was enjoying a quiet swim, at our expense. Jordi immediately reacted by approaching him with a heavy stick which he always keeps just inside the ornate cast iron entrance gates. He sent him packing back over the boundary fence from whence he came.

I was perplexed to hear all of this over the telephone. This was quite a mystery. Who was this old man helping himself to the facilities at our expense?

I assured Jordi that I had not invited any guests to the *casa* and I had certainly not given permission for anyone to enter and use our swimming pool. Were this to happen again, he was to call the *policia municipal*, the local police, in Valldemossa.

The mystery was solved on my return to the island. We have no close neighbours, save for a retired American judge who owns the nearest house to us, out of sight and several hundred metres away, around the mountainside. He popped over to see me to explain the incident.

"Mea culpa!" he exclaimed. "I've lived here for over 30 years, and it has always been the custom for neighbours to use the facilities of nearby houses. I'd received permission many years ago to enjoy a swim in your pool. Then the previous owner of your house, a German banker, erected goat-proof fencing, barring my passage. I thus climbed over the pool wall and helped myself, thinking this would be in order."

Well, he was told politely, but firmly, that he would be unwise to continue the custom, as the original permission was given three owners ago and Jordi will not entertain any strangers entering upon our land in this manner. Moreover, he is most likely to use excessive force to evict uninvited strangers. He also owns a licensed shot gun, largely to despatch wayward goats which are themselves no respecters of boundaries, and he'd be most unwise to put this to the test should he continue to bathe in our pool naked or otherwise when the urge takes him.

I am not only pleased to report that the incident, at least to my knowledge, has never been repeated, but that both the American and I are regular tennis partners. We happen to meet on court in the grounds of a Deià hotel each week-end when I visit the island and am able to slip away for a social game.

I am not brave enough to impart this information however to Jordi. He would take it as a personal slight and make *me* feel disloyal!

Chapter 3 Sheffield

This city's name is derived from the River Sheaf which runs through its centre. You could be forgiven for missing it. It's hardly a Thames or even a Derwent. But Steel City, as Sheffield was once nicknamed, had by the early 1600's become the main centre for the manufacturing of cutlery in England. It continued to develop a better quality of steel including stainless steel as well as the process of silver plating which became well known throughout the world as Sheffield Plate.

During the Second World War and in common with other English industrial cities, including Birmingham and Coventry, Sheffield was "blitzed" by the Luftwaffe. During a clear frosty night in December 1940 much of its city centre was destroyed.

My own childhood in this South Yorkshire industrial city in the North of England, was tough. Thankfully I had caring, loving parents who thought nothing of sacrificing their own pretty frugal lifestyle in order to give me, their only child, a grammar school education and financial support for a further three years whilst I attended a full-time course at college. This was to elevate me out of a dire working class environment.

I was born just 4 months after D Day in a Victorian end-terraced dwellinghouse which my parents rented from a private landlord. It had a single living room-cum-kitchen on the ground floor, with a bedroom on each of the upper two floors. I remember my father lighting the gas lights, each day at dusk, before conversion to electricity in about 1950. A single cold water tap fed the deep earthenware sink, converted around that time from an iron pump adjoining the outside wall.

The privy was in a brick built terraced row across the yard, ours being No. 13, the "Daily Mirror" and the "Sheffield Star" doubling as both reading material and toilet paper. We would now describe that as 'recycling'!

Rather like the way we would save the silver milk bottle tops and rinsed them before they were thread on a line of string to use as Christmas trimmings along with twirls of red crepe paper.

In the living room was a blackened iron stove with a back boiler which served to produce all our hot water. The coal fire was always roaring on weekly bath nights, when the portable tin bath would come out of a corner. Our clothes, however, would be washed and ironed weekly by mum at the local public washhouse adjoining the slipper baths.

A toasting fork heavy with burnt soot stood alongside the iron stove, testament to the enormously blissful side benefit of having the ability to toast slices of bread on an open fire. Thankfully electric toasters had not then been invented so we were not to realise until much later how lucky we were. Bread toasted with the aid of electricity doesn't come near! Not to mention the rare treat of having roasted chestnuts at Christmas or on bonfire night along with freshly made treacle toffee.

I recall mum bringing in a chimney sweep once a year. Chimney fires were frequent, caused by hot sparks flying up the chimney on the draught created by the open fire. The amount of soot which came down into our living room was incredible.

Coal was delivered in hessian sacks, dropped into a cellar. Frequently I was sent to scavenge along the adjoining railway line for blocks of coal which had fallen from the over laden coal wagons being transported from the nearby Yorkshire, Derbyshire and Nottinghamshire mines to the multitude of steelworks juxtaposed in Sheffield's heavy industrial areas of Attercliffe, Tinsley and Darnall. This was a dangerous occupation. I remember the day our industrial village of Wincobank went solemnly quiet. I must have been about 6 or 7. My distant cousin was out gathering coal from the railway line when he was hit by a passing steam powered express train, and killed instantly.

Such a tragedy failed however to dampen my enthusiasm for train spotting. As often as I could during the mid 1950's when my Junior School was closed for the 6 weeks' summer holidays, I would cycle out of Wincobank towards Brightside. Armed with my jam or cheese sandwich, some water and my Ian Allen train-spotter's book, I found solitude on a steep grassy bank looking down onto the expansive railway line, directly opposite the signals which in those days were mechanical.

This famous stretch of railway was known as Wincobank Junction. I still have in my study a calendar given to me by a former Archdeacon of Birmingham showing number 60007 "Sir Nigel Gresley" thundering northwards through Wincobank Junction and pulling 14 passenger coaches. I "spotted" this locomotive many times as a child.

Regrettably I was not destined to see number 4953 "Pitchford Hall", a Great Western Region steam engine. We lived in a different region. Many years later I was however to visit Pitchford Hall, a Tudor manor house in Shropshire. Unfortunately I couldn't convince them that I was a long lost relative!

Neither did I "spot" number 5972 of the same class. Back then it was called "Olton Hall". I did however see it on a film much later. Its name had been changed to "Hogwarts Express" and I was told it always leaves from London King's Cross, Platform 9 and three quarters for somewhere called Hogsmeade. A likely story!

I would wait patiently for hours on end for the signal to be raised, always with a noisy vibrant clatter, in hopeful expectation of a "named" express train coming thundering by that I hadn't previously "spotted". I would imagine myself on that mysterious, powerfully built steam train, the engine belching dark grey smoke from its funnel, being carried away to some distant seaside resort. In England, my childhood home in Wincobank couldn't have been further from the sea.

The raised signal would tell me that I had about 5 minutes to ready myself before a train would pass by.

I would recognise the sound an express train would make from almost half a mile away, particularly if pulled by a "Royal Scot" or better still a Class A4 North Eastern locomotive such as number 60022 Mallard which gained the steam world speed record of 126mph in 1938.

Almost to the minute, at 3 o'clock in the afternoon, the "Flying Scotsman" would steam along, coming down from Edinburgh. I would dutifully underline neatly in red biro using my wooden ruler the name and number of the locomotive pulling the express train.

The nostalgic smell of soot lingering in the air long after the engine had passed conjured up those seemingly faraway places such as York and Bournemouth.

These were truly magical moments for a young lad.

Across the yard lived my grandmother. Her home was a terraced house identical to ours, but it backed onto another house which had frontage to Barrow Road. Access to the road from my grandmother's was through a dark entry. These "back to back" houses were eventually bulldozed under the local authority's slum-clearance programme. Much later, in Birmingham, a few similar ones were to be preserved as museum pieces, depicting one product of the 19th century industrial revolution.

My grandmother, too, had an iron grated fireplace. I remember this to my cost. She always had a fire lit on which she boiled a kettle of water for her tea. I would regularly wander over the courtyard to sit and chat with her.

That was after she'd say: "Pu' wud in t' oil." Which clearly meant: "Put the wood in the hole." She was really saying "Close the door."

I was about 6 years old when, on one such occasion, I remember stumbling onto the hot iron grate, tipping boiling hot water over and seriously burning my left leg. Poor grandmother, being beside herself, grabbed a tea towel and rather than pouring cold water on the burn, she wiped it with the tea towel. This whole incident I clearly remember as if it were only yesterday. I try not to notice the scars I carry following this event.

This early childhood to teenage phase of my life was not particularly happy.

I was destined to eventually only grow to 5ft 6in. I was just about the smallest boy in my class of 40. Because my parents were relatively poor I had very little, if any, pocket money. My school dinners were sometimes sacrificed for a bread roll bought from a little terraced shop opposite the school with a packet of crisps I stuffed in the middle having first eaten the dough.

My mother also baked bread weekly. It would be left to cool outside on our living room windowsill. This overlooked the courtyard where all the children would congregate to play football or cricket, improvising by chalking goal posts or stumps on the wall to the terraced lavatories.

Once a week we would buy pikelets from a man wearing an apron who would be selling them on the street from his basket on the front of his bicycle. My mother would occasionally send me to buy half a dozen.

The nice man would say to me: "Ooo, you 'ave shot up." Or "Don't eight 'em all thi' sen or tha'll feel sick."

We'd have them toasted by the open fire with lashings of margarine and jam. Most people would know these as crumpets. Delicious.

Because our house had no direct road access, our address was 5 Court 13, Barrow Road, located by the side of a railway line in the shadow of two gasometers. The number 5 referred to the number of the yard onto which our house faced, 13 being the number of the house in this particular yard. The gas street lights were always lit manually at dusk by a man carrying a tall ladder.

The River Don, forming the geographical boundary between Sheffield and Rotherham, was nearby. I remember paddling here, avoiding rusty iron bikes cast off and thrown into the water by their owners, into which ran industrial oily effluent from the nearby steelworks in one of which my father worked as a precision engineer. He proudly made it to middle management eventually, overseeing men making carbide tips for power drills.

During World War II he was not allowed to enlist. Dad was required to continue working in a factory, making parts of aircraft engines for Wellington bombers. At the end of each 12 hour shift he would double as a Home Guard, patrolling around the Edgar Allen Steelworks in Attercliffe Common. The platoon was required to share 5 rifles between 12 men, none of which had any ammunition, dad told me much later with a cheeky grin! It was a good job the Germans didn't invade us!

Sundays were always special. I would be taken early to Sunday school held in a Methodist chapel close to home. This was followed by an 11:00am service. I must have been a model child, for I was presented with an illustrated Holy Bible by the Wincobank Methodist Church for good attendance in 1952. My certificate was marked "1st Class".

I clearly have my parents to thank for that!

A full Sunday lunch would be cooked, always with my mum's tasty Yorkshire pudding and gravy being served up as the first course, regardless of which meat was coming next. This was to fill us up so that we wouldn't need to eat as much meat as we might otherwise want. Today when I have roast beef I will always insist on having the Yorkshire served first.

We would then sit around the "radiogram" listening to Forces Favourites which was later to become "Family Favourites" presented by Jean Metcalf and her husband Cliff Michelmore, music requests dedicated to our forces serving in the B.A.O.R., British Army on the Rhine, followed by "The Glums" or "Hancock's Half Hour" and later "Sing Something Simple" by the Cliff Adams Singers. The Sunday afternoon "Billy Cotton Band

Show" which opened with the cry of "Wakey wakey!" was a real favourite.

The "radiogram" was an enormous piece of wooden furniture housing both a radio and turntable enabling us to play dad's Mario Lanza or Ronnie Ronalde's wax records. A real family occasion, followed, for me at least, by an afternoon nap.

Dad was particularly fond of Ronnie Ronalde. Ronnie was a music hall performer, born in London. He became popular in the late 1940's and 1950's for his yodelling, whistling and bird impressions. "If I were a Blackbird" in 1950 is one of his famous songs.

I remember my father whistling this many times in front of packed audiences during the early 1950's at the Wincobank Working Men's Club. There he also played the drums for the acts that would appear weekly. I suppose it was good pocket money for him, supplementing his wages to see I was properly educated. He was really talented. He seemed popular with the packed audiences and I was so proud of him.

Each year the Club would pay for the local children to go on a day's outing to the seaside. It was usually to Cleethorpes or Bridlington. We would be given name tabs to wear on our lapels along with the number of the charabanc or coach we were allocated to travel on. Usually there would be 9 charabancs and we'd all try and rush to get on the first three as they would set off first. Before we boarded, the driver would announce: "If ya want t' gu tu't lav gu nah cuz wi' not stoppin'."

Bags of plain Smith's crisps each containing a little blue bag of salt would be handed out on the journey along with a bottle of Vimto and some pocket money to spend on amusements and to buy fish and chips for our "dinner".

"Don't loyse it." we would be told.

On the return journey the driver would say: "Wi'll no't bi stoppin', we're gooin' straight 'ooerm."

When nearing home tired but happy we'd all sing "For he's a jolly good driver…"

As a child those trips to me were magical. Much later, as a Chartered Surveyor in Birmingham, I was to return to professionally value the "Wonderland" amusement centre fronting the Cleethorpes promenade where I had spent many an hour on the one-penny slot machines during those outings.

I had a Godfather called Bert Sellers. He ran a local coach business from nearby Standon Road but I recall he had a friend, Gordon Norville, who was an actor. I remember him visiting our house once, dressed as the Green Devil, a role he played, and frightened me to death. This friend was appearing in a pantomime, playing Alderman Fitzwarren in Jack Whittington, at the Lyceum Theatre, Sheffield during the winter of 1952/53. My parents bought me an autograph book having been told that this friend could persuade all the company taking part to sign it.

Looking through it when writing this account I noted the signature of the famous comedian Ken Platt who played

Idle Jack, along with Tony Heaton (Selina the cook) and, can you believe, Morecambe and Wise, who were playing the Captain and Mate, signing their names across a black and white stage photo of themselves and sending me their best wishes. Maybe this autograph book is now worth a few bob.....

Mum, on the other hand, always had a gift for writing poetry. During the later stages of her long life she penned quite a few poems. Such was the passion she managed to evoke in her writings that my son Simon gathered these together and hopes one day to arrange their publication.

As for myself, though not a journalist, I would quite enjoy publishing a best seller or, better still a TV series along the lines perhaps of Peter Mayle's "A Year in Provence" produced in the 1990's. Maybe I can thank my mother for any modicum of literary talent lurking inside. She was certainly a prolific scribe, either of poems or in penning heartfelt letters to her friends.

Anyway, not being a professional writer may not necessarily be a disadvantage. After all, just how many decent literary works have actually been penned by those who should know how to write? Arguably not that many.

How perceptive was Benjamin Disraeli who said, or at least he was attributed to having said back in the 19th century: "When I want to read a novel I write one."

I often wonder just where my parents' careers may have led had they been born in more fortunate circumstances. Only much later did I begin to feel especially humble that they spent much of their lives encouraging me to study, thus enabling me to pursue opportunities as they were presented.

I was a sickly child, to be struck with both asthma and eczema when only three years old. My mother told me later that this illness started one wet summer after we'd camped in a caravan in Bridlington, or was it Cleethorpes?

On reflection I think it was more likely to have been caused by our living adjacent to two enormous gasometers and to my breathing in the escaping toxic gas fumes along with the air polluted from the numerous foundries nearby which proliferated on this side of Sheffield. A cocktail with a kick. Fresh air was certainly in low supply in Wincobank!

In those days everyone had a ration book. I vividly recall as a small boy handing this up over the counter to the local newsagent, tobacconist and sweets shopkeeper who would remove a stamp in exchange for handing over some sweets. The immediate post-war years were indeed austere.

Our annual summer holiday alternated mainly between Mrs Briggs' boarding house in Blackpool one year and Grimsby the next, at my Great Aunt Alice's house backing onto Grimsby Docks, where the air was forever rancid with the smell of the day's catch. We would catch the bus to go a mile down the road into Cleethorpes to watch the latest B movie western my dad and I were so fond of, usually starring Roy Rogers, Randolph Scott, Hopalong Cassidy or Ronald Reagan. Reagan incredibly was to become the 40th president of the USA. Who would have believed it back then?

Mum, Dad and I were regular cinema goers. Well, in Wincobank in the late 1940's and 1950's, well before we could afford a television set, there was very little else by way of amusement. Reading by gaslight was not conducive to good eyesight, so my parents would take me off to see the latest film at Wincobank Palace, palace being something of a misnomer!

Invariably I would become thirsty during the performance, so, rather than buy me an ice cream tub or a carton of diluted orange juice during the interval, I would be sent home to get myself a glass of water. If a Tarzan film was on starring Johnny Weissmuller then I would run all the way there and back so as not to miss his rendition of an elephant call. A Superman in a loincloth. Absolutely unmissable.

Cowboy films were always being shown during Saturday matinees. The cinema was packed with kids. It was continually rowdy. We cheered the good guys who always wore white Stetsons. The baddies wore black Stetsons and were booed. Well in those days the pictures would be in black and white. Often the projector would break down. In unison we would stamp our feet and shout "Put a penny int' slot."

The Paragon, at the end of the Number 4 bus route at Firth Park, in Sheffield, was another such cinema house, but it had a particular distinguishing feature in that an organ would appear in front of the stage, rising from the floor, a man playing for all he was worth. A posher cinema.

What days!

Thankfully I was lucky enough to pass my 11-plus exams from Wincobank Junior School to Greystones, a well-regarded Secondary Grammar school as it was then described, for boys and girls. Each day during this first year at senior school I would take the Number 4 bus to Sheffield City Centre then catch a tram to the school in Ecclesall. Total journey time of 1 hour. A year later the school closed and I was sent to Rowlinson Technical Grammar School for boys only. The journey to this newly built school at Norton was similar, involving the bus to the city centre then a tram all the way to the terminus at Meadowhead.

The double decker Sheffield tramcars evoke strong childhood memories. Today were they still in service we would unhesitatingly describe them as being iconic. Painted in blue and cream livery, the older ones with mainly wooden seats were real bone-shakers. In fact they shook us so viciously along the entire route that it was impossible to complete our previous night's homework on them, at least neatly, before reaching the terminus.

I remember the conductor would push the seats over upon reaching the terminus so the boarding passengers faced the direction of travel.

Alas, these electric powered paragons of people-movers were taken out of service in October 1960 having been first introduced to Sheffield in 1899. I was in the city centre that rainy night to see my first "x" certificate film, Psycho, showing at the Gaumont Cinema. A procession of the last trams was passing by. Many of us put halfpennies on the steel tracks for the trams to run over, thus presenting us with a lasting memento of this sad occasion.

How short-sighted our rulers were back then!

It was during my senior school boy days that I joined the 61st Wincobank troop of boy scouts. Scouting became my principal hobby. I still have my membership card and progress record from 1955. On the back page is written *"Our Founder's Rules for Keeping Fit and Scout-like."*

I thought it might be interesting to record these here, as they aptly demonstrate a personal code of daily life at that time:

"Every evening clean your teeth.
Sleep 8 hours every night and keep your windows open.
Try to get a bath or rub down with a wet towel every morning.
Do scout exercises and breathing before breakfast.
At night ask God's forgiveness for any unscoutlike acts during the day past, and give thanks for good things enjoyed.
In the morning pray for strength to do your best in the coming day.
Every day do a good turn, no matter how small, to someone."

Almost 60 years on I like to think such rules are still apposite.

We hiked all over the Peak District every weekend. I learned how to tie knots, cook a rabbit in a clay oven we made in the woods, learnt morse code and practiced first aid. Proficiency badges were awarded to be proudly worn on the sleeve. This was enjoyable, though going off to summer camp I invariably had pretty bad attacks of asthma which occasionally meant I had to return home.

I have a vivid recollection of the time in 1956 aged 12 when I was taken to my first boy scout Jamboree, held in Sutton Coldfield near Birmingham in the Midlands. I had begun learning French at school and recall practising certain phrases I'd proudly learnt to a couple of unsuspecting boy scouts from France. God knows what they were thinking when I came out with *"Qu'est-ce que c'est?"* pointing at a pen knife one of them was holding.

My wonderful parents had kitted me out well, and bought me a pair of lederhosen shorts as part of my scout uniform. Now, you may not believe this, but I still wear those same leather shorts today, whilst gardening in our place in Majorca, some 55 years on! In all that time, I have only needed to replace the zip and then only last year. Money well spent eh?

Progressing, first to patrol leader and then to senior scout, I suspect this experience gave me the confidence to get through my adolescent years and prepared me well for my three years at college which were to become some of the best years of my life.

My life was to change when I joined a full-time degree course in estate management at the local College of Technology, now Sheffield Hallam University. My parents were unable to afford to send me to the College of Estate Management in London where I really preferred to go, before the CEM was to move to Reading University. It had the highest reputation.

My course had just been introduced in Sheffield and in the month of May in each of the three years we had to travel by train to Leeds where we were required to sit for the external examinations of the Royal Institution of Chartered Surveyors.

We stayed a week in a boarding house in Crossgates, struggling with our drawing boards and T- squares on trains and buses. What fun! It's a good job we were all intent on passing. We could so easily have been diverted. We very nearly were, as a new pop group called the Beatles had just had a sensational Top 20 hit with their first single, "Love Me Do" which they quickly followed with "Please Please Me".

Happily I somehow passed each year's examinations at the first attempt and qualified as a Chartered Valuation Surveyor at the age of 21.

Supping frothy coffee, as students in Sheffield did in those days, in the Sidewalk Cafe in Chapel Walk, I was approached by an older guy in his early 20's.

"What are you doing this afternoon?" he enquired

"I'm attending a lecture on Economics." I replied

"Oh, that sounds boring," he said, "would you like to come back to my place, it's very comfortable? I have a lovely settee in the front lounge, I can draw the curtains and we can watch a film."

My naivety nearly led me into this trap. It was my college friend who told me he was gay, as we now call homosexuals, and that this was his chat up line.

I can remember running all the way to the college in Pond Street, arriving early for my tutorial. That was a first!

Well, don't get me wrong; I've got nothing against the gay community, but remember back then this whole area of sexual proclivity was considered taboo. I was spooked. It wasn't even legal at that time. It was swept under the carpet and society tried to shun it. Thankfully we have learned to moderate our attitude and the law and society in general now seem to accept this as a matter of course.

Thinking back, maybe I should have taken the proposition as a compliment!

The 1960's era was outstanding in all respects.

I was especially keen on the Beatles, the Rolling Stones and the Searchers. The Esquire Jazz Club was a must place to be every Friday night, often with all-night sessions of jazz or rhythm and blues often with Dave Berry, Joe Cocker or Georgie Fame on the bill along with American R & B icons such as Muddy Waters, Sonny Boy Williamson and Howlin' Wolf.

Chris Spedding, my wife's brother, was beginning his long professional career as a song writer and guitarist. He was to compose and sing "Motorbikin"', a top 10 hit in the UK singles charts in the 1970's before he took off to New York and then LA.

His illustrious career, following the heady 60's and 70's era of drugs, sex and rock 'n roll, led him to play with such stars as Paul McCartney, Katie Melua, David Essex, Roxy Music and Bryan Ferry. He was to produce and manage the Sex Pistols during the punk rock era and somewhat incongruously was a founder member of the Wombles with Mike Batt.

Chris still plays lead guitar occasionally for Bryan Ferry, features sometimes in Roxy Music reunion gigs and plays lead guitar in Jeff Wayne's epic "War of the Worlds". Check out his web site www.chrisspedding.com.

After qualifying and working in Sheffield for a year I decided to finally make a break from living with my parents. I had become engaged and it was an obvious time to fly the nest. I simply opened a map of England and decided where I wanted to work.

Today that would be unthinkable. I decided that it wouldn't be London but somewhere not too far away from my parents and my fiancée.

Birmingham was thriving. It was within easy driving distance from Sheffield. So I applied to a couple of firms, received offers from both, settled on one and so started my career in earnest. The rest, as they say is history.

The swinging 60's. By far the best decade I can recall.

Chapter 4 Bernardo

"Una pregunta, por favour." Bernardo, a recently retired village postman, wanted to ask me a question.

We were gathered at Jordi's for lunch. Bernardo, Tony-con-barba, (the bearded Tony, to differentiate from other locals named Tony, Jordi and me. I'd been asked to arrive at 1pm precisely. That's when the main electronic gate off the Valldemossa-Deià road would open to admit me.

Unusual, for a Spaniard, but Jordi was anything but usual. For example, when he says he'll be up at ours for 7.30am to attend to our pool, that's precisely the time he arrives.

Recently I noticed a thin coating of yellow dust appearing on the side walls to the swimming pool. I grabbed a brush and after a 20 minute sweaty workout the walls were spotlessly clean. Regrettably for me, however, the pool had turned *turbio*, murky. Upon Jordi's arrival he couldn't understand what had turned his crystal clear pool cloudy. Until, that is, I admitted that I'd cleaned the sides.

In excitable poor Spanish, Jordi set about telling me off for touching his pool – which is really my pool. And, remember, he works for me, not the other way around! He fixed the problem by throwing some chemicals into the pool, telling me not to touch it again. Everything is done by eye and nose. Jordi's law.

He's yet to discover I've bought an electronic testing kit (though haven't yet worked out how to use it). My real test is how I can persuade Jordi to adopt it as a useful aid to his work without him throwing a very Spanish tantrum!

"Una pregunta, por favour."

I turned attentively to Bernardo who calls me Glynny, pronounced Gleenee as opposed to Jordi who also cannot pronounce my name and settles for either *Senor Picfor* or *el Ingles*.

He wanted to know how much Viagra costs in England.

Well, Bernardo has fallen in love, after having been divorced some 20 years ago since when he's never become attached to anyone else. He took retirement last year at age 60, and, it transpired, he's now bitten off a little more than he can chew. He is a suave, taller than your average Majorcan, with a thick mop of silver hair and a spitfire pilot's moustache. He has met a diminutive Paraguayan with a rather excessive sexual appetite. Please excuse me if I say he can't keep it up!

"Four pills cost me €98." he exhorts. He was asking me if I could investigate and, if cheaper, bring him a supply on my next island visit.

On the grounds that discretion was the better part of valour I declined from suggesting he might be wiser in adopting a more ascetic approach to his predicament!

It's difficult to imagine such an explicit conversation around a British dining table. For all their localism they do seem more worldly, the Spanish.

When I did enquire back home with my friend Mike, a retired doctor, I learned that Viagra was indeed considerably cheaper in England – the catch was that one needs a doctor's prescription to obtain them. There was no way this was going to happen. And anyway how was I going to explain to the Customs Officer that I'm bringing over a year's supply of Viagra when I am on the island for only 2 weeks!

If this is the price of true love, maybe Bernardo should watch more television.

All's well that ends well, however. Or maybe not! Happenstance played its timely part.

I was relaying this tale to a fellow guest at Doctor Mike's house. As the dinner party was in full swing this particular guest, who happened to be a nurse, mentioned she had 18 such tablets in her bedside drawer. I suppose they were there as a sort of insurance policy! But, happily for Bernardo, I gladly accepted them as she felt she would no longer have use for them, her new partner clearly proving to be most adequate in that department.

A packet arrived by post just one day before we were due to bring out our two grandchildren for their annual summer holiday with us. The parcel contained four tablets, the others, I suspect, kept locked away for a few rainy days.

On returning to the island I eagerly anticipated relating this tale to Jordi and plotting how these might be handed over to Bernardo. Here's where I made a big mistake, according to my wife. My error was in handing over the package to Jordi and not directly to his friend Bernardo.

That morning I couldn't wait to show them to Jordi who took them from me for his friend. We went off in my hired car to Valldemossa to buy bread and sup coffee in the local bar, chatting about how these might be transferred to Bernardo when we see him in the week. Jordi was having great fun at Bernardo's expense, saying that at his age, now turned 61, he should not be needing such an aid to his sexual prowess.

We returned to our *casa* to receive the water lorry which Jordi had arranged. It was to deliver some 12,000 litres to see us through the next few weeks. Mains water is merely a distant dream in these mountains. The plot fell apart when I received a telephone call from a rather desperate Jordi who, by now, had returned to his home nearby.

"Que pasa?" "What's happened?" I asked, trying to calm him down so that I could attempt to understand at least one in three of his words and piece together the reason for the call.

"Have I got the package there?" asked Jordi.

"No," I replied, "unfortunately I gave it to you here before we went up to the village. Why?"

He had misplaced, possibly lost, the package. It was my turn to throw a fit.

"Estas loco!" I told him. "You're stupid!"

My thoughts turned to the package containing the 4 Viagra tablets. They were in a brown jiffy bag, the same bag which my friend the nurse had posted to me and which bore my UK name and address, clearly typed on the front!

I whisked him back to the village to retrace our steps. He had to ask the barman Clemente and the lady assistant in the *panaderia*, the bakery. In the time I have known Jordi I have never seen him so embarrassed. He was reluctant to confront the lady *panadera* until I forced him. He was blushing all over his face, and rightly so.

We didn't find them.

I had terrible thoughts that someone may have mistaken the parcel for a bomb and that the police would be calling on me. Better they were found by an honest English tourist and posted back to my UK address. But there aren't too many caring people about, so I thought maybe that this was unlikely to happen. And it didn't!

I recalled the doctrine in tort that imposes responsibility upon one person for the failure of another. It's called "vicarious liability". I wondered: who could sue whom? By this time I was getting into a pickle!

Both Jordi and my wife blame me for Jordi's ineptitude. It's an unjust world! So we concocted a story for Bernardo, oblivious as yet to this incident as we hadn't seen him. Bernardo elected to receive the good news ahead of the bad news.

Jordi had phoned Bernardo and told him that he needed to receive some personal news which could not be told over the telephone. To receive it Bernardo called on Jordi in the local bar.

"Buenas noticias," good news, Jordi said to Bernardo. "El ingles has been able to source some Viagra tablets for you."

His face lit up. Bernardo's greying handle bar moustache rose to the occasion.

"There are conditions." he was told. His moustache drooped. "You will owe Senor Picfor here a cafe americano with a whisky," Jordi exclaimed when we both went up to Valldemossa one early morning to buy our daily bread and deliver the good news. His moustache stiffened and his eyes shone brightly.

"But," Jordi said, "as we have only 4 tablets, they will have to last you a few weeks."

Readers will recall that to buy 4 Viagra tablets, from the village pharmacist with a doctor's prescription, costs

Bernardo 98 euros. "You must therefore use them sparingly."

I suggested that he does not swallow the first tablet, but lick it, and have a peek at his manhood. "Lick and peek, lick and peek." I said. "When the action commences be sure to put the tablet back in its packet. That way, they will last you a few more months, thus saving you many euros."

Jordi looked across at me with a beaming smile. I had just recounted what is in effect a joke which the Majorcans tell against the Catalans, people from the region centred around Barcelona.

"Pero, tengo malas noticias." But I had bad news, I told him. "I handed the package to Jordi on my arrival who then promptly lost it, the imbecile."

Once more the moustache drooped, I suspect in sympathy to another part of his anatomy. Nonchalantly Bernardo then responded by telling us that he has now sourced a supply of even stronger tablets by legal prescription, getting 8 tablets for 60 euros monthly.

He shrugged his shoulders at the whole sorry episode but seemed happy enough.

By now it's 1.30pm and a typical Majorcan lunch at Jordi's is being put out – a young pig, roasted for over 4 hours in the outside oven accompanied by *patatas fritas* (cubes of potato fried in olive oil with garlic) and *ensalada mixta*, mixed salad.

It is an honour, apparently, to be served the pigs head. This went to Tony-con-barba, sitting at the head of the table. Thank goodness, I thought, that it wasn't presented to me. I was feeling pretty full after this when the next course was served, *frito mallorquin*, another speciality of Majorca, made from potatoes fried in olive oil with garlic, herbs and red wine to which is added minced meat. Delicious, but not after a full plate of roast suckling pig!

Pudding was almond cake made by Jordi's daughter-in-law from nearby Soller, plus the ubiquitous Majorcan oranges from his orchard. Coffee in glasses too hot to pick up, plus a blended whisky, followed the local red table wine.

The conversation turned to the walk which Bernardo had recently taken me on, with Jordi as the "porter". I say this because Jordi carries far too much weight to be remotely interested in walking up into the mountains though nevertheless on this occasion he agreed to accompany us and proceeded to carry my binoculars and water bottle.

Bernardo was our guide. He knows these mountains like the back of his hand. After all he goes into the mountains most mornings and occasional evenings to set his nets in pre-prepared positions so as to catch mainly *tordos* when the birds fly their nests at daybreak looking for breakfast or as they return at dusk.

Starting from the centre of Valldemossa there is an interesting walk leading to the summit of one of the peaks where a 360 degree vista exposes panoramic views of both the bay of Palma looking south and the village of Deià diametrically opposite, to the north. The path eventually winds its way down the other side of the mountain through a dense pine forest, eventually coming out by our *casa*.

I suppose the route would have taken us about an hour and a half had Jordi not been present and wanting to stop for a rest every few hundred metres.

Jordi's guests had a terrific laugh over this event, at his expense, noting that he had not been walking much since.

By 2.30pm the other guests lifted themselves out of the moulded plastic chairs and bid their farewells. I took the lead and followed suit.

Typical long Spanish lunches are not for Jordi!

Chapter 5 6th July 1968

I first set eyes on Margaret Elizabeth Spedding when, one weekend during my first year in college, a friend called Mont and I gate crashed a party she was having in her home in Grove Road, Millhouses, unbeknown to her parents who had gone away for the weekend.

During my 3 years at college it became customary to find out who was having a party on the following Saturday night, then gate crash! I don't remember ever being turned away. We would first meet up at The Museum. Not a culture fix but a pub in the city centre. I would down a pint of Stone's bitter as quickly as I could to Mont's two or three pints. Well, he was 6 feet 6 inches tall and so had more to fill. This was a pretty cheap way I'd discovered of getting myself merry enough to summon up courage to chat up the girls!

On this occasion once we'd arrived at the family home we helped ourselves to draft ale, directly out of the barrel into empty jam jars which doubled as beer mugs! The attic where the party was being held was full of university students and sixth formers. Maggie at the time was one of the latter. She was quite merry after only a half a pint of beer or cider. I was merry on a pint. Thus the gate crashing was easy.

The noise was deafening. Pity the neighbours in this quiet suburban neighbourhood. At full throttle the Beatles' first album was playing. At first, I couldn't help noticing Jane, sat alongside Maggie, but she already had an established boyfriend. She was later to become our chief bridesmaid.

The lights were either off or set low. It was pretty smoky. As the party progressed I was approached by someone who had just passed his entrance exams to Oxford.

"Would you like one of these?" he asked. They were tiny white pills.

"What are they?" I responded.

"Ephedrine tablets, one for a £1."

Well, the reader already knows I have suffered with asthma since childhood. As it so happens in those days before Ventolin inhalers, I was prescribed those same tablets, free of charge. I didn't carry them about me; they were a strong medication. A stimulant which speeds up the heart. But I needed some Dutch courage if I were ever to chat up the fair hostess. So, I bought one tablet and downed it with a beer. Not to be recommended, and absolutely never tried again.

It did, however, do the trick. I asked Maggie to dance. Well, that's a euphemism for a smooch, seeing as there was no room in that attic to be anywhere other than close up and personal. Very personal! That first kiss seemed to last an age. We were oblivious to all the pushing and shoving going on where others were stomping wildly to the music. When we both came up for air who would have realized that we were about to embark upon a relationship which was to last to this present day?

So maybe, just maybe, it was a pound well spent.

A week or two later I got to meet the parents.

Maggie's father was a Bank Manager. He looked after the Sheffield Wednesday account so I was in awe from the start. He played the piano rather well and Maggie's mother was a Pharmacist. I soon learned that in front of her mother, Maggie, who was really a tom-boy at heart, was addressed as Margaret. Her Bach choir-singing mum was quite a strict lady! As a lad from Wincobank though by now living on the Gleadless Valley estate in Sheffield I soon realised I had to watch my "p's" and "q's" or I reckoned I'd be out on my ears.

As a member of the National Union of Students I was able to gain entry into the University of Sheffield students' hops every Saturday night. To save entrance fees I would arrange to meet Maggie inside as she'd also joined a full-time course in Institutional Management at my college and had become a member of the Students Union. I know, this was really mean! But she didn't seem to mind.

Another big plus in my favour was that Maggie wasn't expensive to take out on account of how quickly she got tipsy which, from my Yorkshire perspective, was an asset.

We must have seen pretty much most of the leading pop groups of the 1960's at these events.

Before meeting Maggie I recall one occasion when I was at such a hop with my cousin Roy who was also a musician. Student nurses were coached into Sheffield from nearby Nottingham for the live band experience. Then, I recall, girls outnumbered the boys in Nottingham by a factor of 3. It was likened by the guys to knocking down skittles with a football! Having just passed my driving test, I asked Roy if I could borrow his mini van to drive a girl I'd met back home to Nottingham. "No problem" said Roy, and gave me the car key. No breathalysers in those days! Not that I was drunk, please note.

Unfortunately, and to my great embarrassment, I was unable to locate the ignition, whereupon I had to return to the hop, find Roy and receive instructions on how to start this vehicle. Remember this was well before the invention of mobile phones. Of course, I now know it's located on the floor between the driver and passenger. A really weird place to put a starter button.

I understood why, upon my return to the car, my passenger had disappeared, deciding to take the coach back home!

I was obviously destined to be unlucky in those days with regard to the fairer sex. Following an all-nighter at the Esquire Jazz Club I arranged to meet the following day a girl I had met that previous evening. Upon arriving at the appointed hour the shock of seeing her in broad daylight was unsettling. She was not at all how I had remembered her. After all it was pretty dark in the club and I'd had a drink or two!

My expectations having been severely dashed I regret I behaved very badly. I excused myself from the date, saying that I needed to take the bus home immediately to tend to my sick mum. For the next couple of weeks I gave the Esquire a wide birth!

I began to be more serious towards Maggie.

I'd still arrange to meet her inside the Union hops to avoid paying for her but our relationship was becoming steady. I proposed to her at yet another party in Dronfield in 1965. I still recall her wearing a turquoise fitted dress bought from Wallis' and worn just above her knees with buttons covered in the same material. She was a slip of a thing and we were chatting, she on my lap in a room full of people the music playing loud in the background. We were balancing jam jars of beer. There were plentiful supplies of jam jars in South Yorkshire and for that matter Derbyshire in those days!

I got to feeling quite nostalgic and decided there and then to ask her to marry me.

Well, after she said yes I then worked out what I needed to say to her father to gain his permission.

By then Mr and Mrs Spedding had retired to a new bungalow in the Peak District. I was due there for Sunday lunch. An opportune time.

Maggie kept her mum chatting in the kitchen while I summoned up the courage to ask her father for his only daughter's hand in marriage. Just like in the films. Happily after proffering some advice as to how he felt I should treat his daughter he consented. There, the deed was done and the road map for a future together set out.

We were married in 1968 in a quaint village Church in Curbar, near Chatsworth House in the Peak District of Derbyshire, close to Calver to where my in-laws were now living, the meandering River Derwent passing close by.

I was in danger of being late for my own wedding.

Well, the Peak District has numerous picturesque inns and, as it so happened, one such inn, the Bridge Inn, was located just across from the church in Curbar. We had invited a few friends from Bristol, London and Basingstoke. I had been boarding with them in Birmingham before some of them became my tenants when my wife-to-be and I bought a modern semi-detached house off Middleton Hall Road in a suburb known as Kings Norton. It paid our mortgage. Maggie was completing her course back in Sheffield.

They were still in occupation on our wedding day but promised faithfully that they would vacate before we returned from our honeymoon. What a risk that was. The Bristolians in particular were quite mad, lived the highlife incorporating booze, sex and rock 'n roll, unlike me, still a pretty naïve shy person from "up north". They soon changed that, though to this day I still have a low threshold when drinking alcohol.

A condition of these friends continuing to reside in the nuptial home was that without fail they would re-decorate the lounge before moving out just one day before we returned to start our new life together in Brum.

So there we all were, supping in the Bridge Inn, when my "best man" Peter, a close friend from college and a bit of a worrier, dashed in to tell me the wedding car had arrived and Maggie was getting out of the car. With that news I rushed by her and straight into church. The vicar looked a bit worried but I wasn't late, technically.

It was the 6th July 1968. That evening we were seen off by the wedding guests to spend the night in Cambridge prior to catching a flight the following morning to Ibiza. Immediately we had "escaped" we pulled up in the next village for fish and chips – we were ravenous, not having eaten much over the wedding celebrations. Not too glamorous but when needs must...

Happily, and to our enormous relief, or mine more accurately, our carefree friends kept their side of the bargain and had vacated our new home but only just prior to our return.

We were to begin our new lives together in Birmingham.

Author, 4th from left on his
wedding day, 6th July 1968.

Sketch of author by Brendan McMahon

Chapter 6 Sport

My earliest recollection of being interested in sport was when I was about 8. As we lived nearer to Hillsborough, home of Sheffield Wednesday Football Club rather than Bramall Lane where Sheffield United plays, my Dad took me to most of the home games. The terraces were packed. We would stand in the Kop, no seats in those days, and I invariably would see much of the game perched on dad's shoulders. Much later I well remember the occasion when the "Owls", as they are nicknamed, hosted Barcelona and we won 4-2.

One of our close neighbours and friends of my parents were the Dooleys. Their son Derek played centre forward for the Owls and became the club's most prolific goal scorer. His career was cut short in 1953 when following a serious accident during his last game for Sheffield Wednesday his leg was amputated. I vividly recall seeing him hobbling around Wincobank and feeling distraught for him.

Yorkshire County Cricket Club also played some county games in the 1950's at Bramall Lane and occasionally I would sneak into the ground after school, when the gates to the ground were left open, to watch fiery Freddie Trueman, Len Hutton and future England players including Ray Illingworth and Brian Close. Those were the halcyon days for Yorkshire cricket and it was a real joy to see all these stars in action.

Little did I realise that some decades later I was to meet many of these cricketers with others such as Geoffrey Boycott when I became the consultant surveyor to Warwickshire County Cricket Club and attended all the England Test Matches when they played at Edgbaston, watching the match from the committee room where I was to dine at the same table with various international stars. Amazing!

In 1996 England were playing Test matches against India and Pakistan. I was on the Warwickshire committee when Edgbaston was hosting Pakistan for a one-day international match. I was deputed to look after the Pakistan High Commissioner along with dignitaries from the Pakistan consulate and their cricket administration.

We clearly got on well as I was asked if I would like to visit Islamabad. Sounds good, but it never happened!

At that time their country was experiencing a period of political musical chairs. Benazir Bhutto was alternating with Nawaz Sharif as their Prime Minister and Pervez Musharraf was a rising star in the army prior to becoming the country's President. The invitation to me never came. I suspected some of those I was entertaining had disappeared in some coup! It was suggested to me I think mischievously by some members of the Warwickshire committee that they had probably been shot!

My one other disappointment was not persuading Shane Warne, the former Australian leg spinner to sign his name on my wide-brimmed cricket hat which I use in my office to tune in to BBC Radio's Test Match Special, the hat being fitted with a radio! The hat is full of autographs from people famous in the cricketing world, both players and commentators.

Alas, Warnie's agent stepped in and declined the opportunity when playing in an England v. Australia Test match at Edgbaston to get me his client's signature. I came to realise some things are not possible without inducement! He wanted payment which cut against the grain. Warnie was kept away from us so I never did get to ask him personally.

I also love to play tennis. At the age of eleven I taught myself by hitting a ball for hours on end against the gable wall of our end terraced house, above the bike shed.

I'd chosen tennis as my summer sport when I started grammar school, chosing to play rugby in the winter. I needed to keep up with the other boys so I was determined to practice. When I moved to Birmingham I joined Kings Norton Tennis Club since when I've been a member of numerous clubs, depending on where Maggie and I moved to.

Decades later, at my present tennis club in Solihull, my coach Matt is tearing out his hair trying to break down my unorthodox strokes and re-fashion them into how I should be playing. My current losing streak is egging me on to get through this and to change my game just sufficiently so that I might start winning more games than I am currently losing. I live in hope though this could be misplaced!

It was during this period that I also took to playing squash and later racquetball, that is until my knees started playing up.

As a boy skiing was not yet on my radar. In fact my first overseas holiday was not until I turned 15, when my parents saved enough money to send me on a school trip to Imperia, on the Italian Riviera close to the French border. We travelled by train, steam in 1959, exciting but sooty and the journey took an age.

Around this time I developed a passion for caving. Potholing, as it used to be called. A number of interesting well known caves are to be found in Derbyshire's Peak District National Park. Three or four of us would change into boiler suits, don pit helmets with battery-powered lights and set off deep down into the bowels of the Peak District. We only went with experienced guides. We would climb down narrow crevices inside the cave, crawl along on our bellies and wade through underground ponds and water courses.

What an experience. Not, perhaps, for my parents, but certainly for me at that time.

In Birmingham, whilst involved on regional committees for the Royal Institution of Chartered Surveyors, I was to lead a team on three separate occasions on what is called the 24 hour 3 Peaks Walk. We had to climb the three highest mountains in Scotland (Ben Nevis), England (Scafell Pike) and Wales (Snowdon) all within 24 hours, starting and finishing at sea level.

Back in 1976 this interesting challenge was not as widely known as it is today. I therefore wrote to Sir Edmund Hilary who had conquered Mount Everest in 1953 and he replied confirming his willingness to act as our advisor.

I recall his famous quote when, with Sherpa Tenzing, he was descending Everest following his successful ascent: "Well, we knocked the bastard off!"

He sent me a lovely letter with some useful tips.

Stamina training was vital. I allocated different team members to "recce" the 3 mountains. My responsibility was to familiarise the Scafell Pike routes and decide which we would take during the gruelling event. Timing would be crucial as we needed to arrive just pre-dawn and begin the ascent whilst it was still dark.

During the Easter prior to the climb I decided to camp with Maggie and our friends Mike and Jenny who knew the Lake District pretty well. By the time we arrived on the camp site it was a moonless night. We couldn't see a thing and we were tired. We hurriedly pitched our 4-man tent and tried to settle down. Imagine our surprise when we popped our heads outside the tent the following morning to find we had inadvertently pitched it virtually overlapping that of our neighbour's. Our neighbour was not a happy man and accused us of pitching it so close to his tent that it made his effectively semi-detached!

Personally I think he was unreasonable, but we quickly moved our tent a few yards further away from his.

Easter, it so happened that year, was in March. Do you realise how cold it can be sleeping under canvas at that time of year? Frost lay on the ground, it seemed both inside the tent as well as outside! We donned layer upon layer of clothing before tucking into our sleeping bags and left the cooking stove on through the night. My wife still can't believe how I managed to persuade her to sleep under canvas for a couple of sharp bitterly cold nights that early Easter!

We spent the weekend climbing Scafell Pike three times before I was satisfied as to the quickest route to take.

In the case of Scotland we would start the clock from sea level at Fort William, stopping it on arrival in Caernarfon in Wales. The walkers, in teams of 4, would be driven by experienced volunteers between the mountains. Each vehicle would be fitted with walkie-talkies and, with police cooperation, would really fly from one mountain area to the next. On each occasion we would undertake the task at the beginning of May. We would encounter rain, hail, fog, blizzards and deep snow on all the mountains.

Needless to say, we were well trained in first aid, were fit and had a sizeable back up team following us providing us with hot food and any other assistance we might have needed. All this to raise funds in aid of various charities. To complete each of these walks as we did in less than 24 hours was particularly satisfying.

As for golf I decided to give it a try since many of my friends played. Unfortunately the ball is quite a bit smaller than a tennis ball and the art is to hit it sweetly along the fairway whilst it is lying stationary. It soon became clear that I was not going to master this strange game. I decided to concentrate on my tennis.

Before we discovered the magical island of Majorca, my interest in sport took a further twist.

Shortly after our moving home to the village of Berkswell I was to join the Round Table movement in nearby Coventry, thanks to my neighbour Terry, a well known solicitor. The family were big rugby fans. I long held an ambition to see England play at Twickenham, and I grabbed the opportunity to go when Terry and his father offered me a place in his party to see England play Ireland. I couldn't wait. Tradition dictated that we would travel to London in a hired Co-op funeral car, suitably laden in its voluminous boot with essential refreshments, all liquid. Certain watering holes were experienced along the route, followed by a heavy mainly liquid lunch in a pub alongside the River Thames at Richmond.

It is with some shame I must report that I was led to my seat in the hallowed ground, to be awakened only by the final whistle. I had slept through the entire match! Some trip.

Alas the lesson was not learnt. Being duly initiated, many such jaunts followed. What is not advisable is to commit to a dinner party afterwards.

I accepted an invitation to see England play the old enemy, Wales. Terry agreed to my one condition: that I would be back in Berkswell by 8pm when I was expected to join my wife and others for dinner at a friend's house.

"No problem", he said, "the match ends at 4.30pm so we'll get you back in time."

Following the mandatory stop in a Cotswold inn I was duly delivered to my host's home at 9pm. Only an hour late!

Terry propped me up at the door, rang the bell then scarpered. The door opened, I threw in my hat then promptly fell into the entrance hall. Being sloshed *before* dinner is definitely not a good idea. Understandably neither the host nor Maggie was amused, but I couldn't stop giggling. Sleep got the better of me between the pudding course and the cheeseboard.

A good few Brownie points were lost that night. Quite properly I was *persona non grata* for a time. The match, however, was a classic!

I enjoyed playing rugby which I started at my senior school at Rowlinson. I still have the school's magazine of Summer 1960 in which there was an annual report of our fourth year team. I was mentioned in these terms:

"We remember their 9 a side battles at Dore Moor when a little fellow, more Pitch than Ford, out-ran, out-jinked a whole team to score one of the tries of the season."

I went on to play for Sheffield Colts before my career finally brought me to the Midlands. It was from our move to Berkswell that Terry asked if I would help him coach the boys at Moorfields, the home of Leamington RFC which had just started a mini-rugby section. As we each had 2 boys from aged 5 to 7 I took up this particular activity. We were to coach the same team from the Under 6's through to the Under 12's remaining undefeated in all our competitive games throughout that time. Testament to this was when we made an entry into the Guinness Book of Records.

We were featured on BBC TV as a curtain raiser at Coundon Road, home of Coventry RFC just before a semi-final of this country's major national rugby union competition. We were to play a corresponding team from Wales, Caerleon who were also unbeaten over these same years. The result was a creditable 3-3 draw.

One particular match has always stuck in my memory, that against the then Under 9's of London Welsh RFC which we played at their ground in the Old Deer Park in Richmond, London.

I was running one touchline, Neil Kinnock whose son was playing for London Welsh, was running the other. The referee was one of theirs. Then, Kinnock was the Shadow Education Minister. He was just as argumentative running the touchline as he was in the House of Commons, continually disagreeing with his own referee.

Pointing this trait out to him afterwards in the clubhouse bar did not go down too well! I wasn't too bothered, we won!

Occasionally our firm would sponsor Moseley RFC at The Reddings. We would invite along a few business colleagues. After the match, when Moseley had lost to Bristol, I told my friend John Duckers, a hapless Moseley supporter, that I could have done better than their fly-half who had failed to kick the ball between the posts.

Well, this was red rag to a bull. Rod Ackrill a local businessman was in the adjoining box. He and Duckers decided to challenge me. They bet me £20 that I couldn't kick the ball over the bar from the 22m. line. Or at least Ackrill did, as Duckers was skint! I was up for that. I marched out onto the pitch, wearing my winklepickers, stole a ball from a child who looked about ready to burst into tears having been robbed by this strange man in a suit, lined up the ball and gave it my best shot.

Very appropriately it landed on top of the crossbar and drunkenly tottered over with nothing to spare.

I duly marched back to claim my winnings.

Cycling is another sport which would interest me more were it not for the constant battle between cyclist and motorist on our country's narrow highways and complex roundabouts. It's not a battle I wish to enjoin as I suspect the chances of the cyclist coming off best are pretty remote. A network of cycle lanes would encourage many of us out of our cars but this does not seem to be on the radar of most local authorities.

So I limit my cycling to the post box at the end of our road and to Solihull Tennis Club, just round the corner.

I particularly enjoy both walking to the railway station some one mile from us and regularly to the centre of Solihull about 10 minutes away on foot.

At least, in some small way albeit, this helps to salve my conscience regarding my carbon footprint!

As a winter break, when I am not visiting Majorca, skiing is another sport I'm pretty passionate about. I discovered this in my mid 30's. My two sons were probably 8 and 10 attending Solihull Junior School, when my wife and I grabbed the opportunity of accompanying the Junior School sports master and his wife on a school trip to Pejo in the Italian Dolomites. One adult could travel free in a party of 10. The deal was that we would help the master, organise the kids and keep them entertained each evening before lights out. Well, I'd soon learned to ski and began taking an extra trip each year to hone my skills on the slopes.

I was introduced to a very English ski resort by a very English friend and work colleague, Richard, who just happened to excel at two sports he enjoyed: tennis and skiing. I have always thought of Richard as being an enigma in his own lifetime, a puzzle waiting to be solved. Or not. Before he first took me to Wengen he clearly thought me unworthy as his travel companion until I had mastered the pronunciation of this Swiss ski resort located in the Bernese Oberland. It would never do if I were to mispronounce the place in the presence of Richard's friends, also very English, who happened to run the Downhill Only Club in Wengen where, it is said, the English first introduced skiing to the world in 1925.

"Wengen", said Richard, "is pronounced Veng'n" – the emphasis on the "n" following a soft "g". He glides down all gradients so effortlessly, reminding me of an orchestral conductor on skis. I suspect he quietly hums to himself the haunting melody found in Elgar's "Pomp and Circumstance"!

It was with Richard, who ran another chartered surveying practice in Birmingham, when the two of us took the longest bubble lift in Europe from Grindelwald up to Mannlichen above Wengen. This takes 35 minutes. By the time we alighted at the top we had cemented a deal between us for bringing his firm into ours. After both of us having cleared the move with our respective partners it then took the lawyers about 3 months to conclude!

Richard and I managed incredibly to win the "Jungfrau Jaunt" cup in 1996 which is an annual Treasure Hunt on skis and great fun, organised by the Ski Club of Great Britain.

After enjoying dinner we generally finished with a coffee and cognac accompanied by a Villiger Swiss-made cigar. I always finished the cigar before Richard. And then he told me his secret as to how it came about that his cigars lasted much longer to smoke than mine.

"Notice my technique, Glyn." He said. "I place my thumb on the end of the cigar, thus restricting the flow of air through it and thus slowing down the burn process!"

Only Richard would think of doing this, and he's not even a Yorkshireman! Needless to say I have adopted this pose whenever I find myself enjoying a decent cigar.

After all these years I still try to make two trips a year, usually to Wengen and Davos, also in Switzerland. The journey from Zurich airport by train to either venue is a real delight.

Readers who have travelled on the Swiss Panoramic train from Lucerne to Interlaken will understand. Skis and luggage can be arranged to be sent ahead from any UK airport, only to be next seen in the chosen resort hotel. This spectacular journey takes you alongside picturesque lakes and over a steep mountain pass, eventually reaching Interlaken, at the junction, as the name suggests, of two lakes. The train's generous seating layout with warm colours creates a wonderful ambience, giving a real incentive to travel by rail. I wish this could be replicated on our railways in the British Isles.

My favourite hotel in Wengen with excellent food and an evening pianist is The Faulken which we all lovingly refer to as Faulty Towers due to its many similarities with the John Cleese tv series. The hotel was built in 1895 and is packed with the luxuries of a sadly bygone era. Rich materials, antique furniture, historical paintings and photos take you back in time through the hotel's history. I always feel relaxed here and feel at home right away.

It is Italian owned and hosts the Italian downhill racing team each January, competing in the famous Lauberhorn race. The shared facilities on the top floor beggar belief, with hot water coming out of the cold water tap and vice versa. But this merely adds to its idiosyncratic charm as a relaxing and friendly place to stay.

On a recent visit I met up with an American in nearby Murren who wanted to ski the world famous downhill race piste. He was with his daughter and asked me for directions. It was only after I'd volunteered to lead them to and ski with them this famous course that I learned he was a ski instructor to the Generals in the US Army, whilst his daughter ran a ski school in Vermont.

Needless to say I was hard pressed top keep up with them, but we ended up skiing together for $1^1/_2$ days at the end of which he politely advised me to buy new skis and new boots if I really wanted to improve my skiing. He also, wisely, suggested I started wearing a helmet. I decided to follow his recommendations.

Wengen is set on a high shelf above the Lauterbrunnen valley, opposite Murren, and can only be reached by cog railway. This is the Jungfrau region, near Interlaken, in the Bernese Oberland. In my view, the prettiest panoramic vistas in the entire Alps are to be found here, with Mount Eiger taking pride of place.

From Kleine Sheidegg, a popular destination above Wengen, a short but steep train journey which tunnels through the Eiger, takes tourists, largely Japanese, up to the Jungfraujoch, which boasts the highest railway station in Europe, some 3454 metres above sea level. Clear skies permitting, the views are really stunning.

Here there is a fascinating palace built of ice. Not surprisingly, this is a UNESCO World Heritage Site.

In Wengen the owner of one of the smaller chalet hotels I stayed in is a model railway enthusiast. One morning he agreed to run his electric trains for us on an elaborate railway system he had built outside the hotel and within its grounds. It had snowed constantly through the night. We awoke to a good foot of the white stuff covering the model railway. I expected that the demonstration would be cancelled.

Silly me, I had momentarily forgotten we were in Switzerland. The owner simply went into his shed and brought out his model locomotive which had attached to it a snow plough. After placing it on the track and weighting down the engine he simply turned on the electric power and sent it on its way, clearing the snow off the lines before setting in motion a number of other locos each having a varying array of goods wagons and passenger coaches. Wonderful.

Only very recently I found it helpful to join the ski club of Great Britain as my wife is not a skier and I rather enjoy going on my own on these winter trips. I have long since abandoned taking both my sons together, as their idea of "après ski" is very different from mine. I never seem to take enough Paracetemol when they accompany me!

I do admit, however, to having enjoyed taking during their Easter holiday in 2011 my two grandchildren, Freya aged 9 and Jack aged 7 on their very first ski trip. We travelled to Flaine in France, along with their father, my younger son Simon. Most enjoyable, notwithstanding the lack of snow and much higher temperatures than normal for this resort.

Unlike the occasion when I was skiing in Davos, with the guide from the Ski Club of Great Britain and Sarah, the rep from the travel company.

Just the 3 of us met for what proved to be an interesting day. We decided to take the long run from the highest peak above Davos towards nearby Klosters but veering off to Kublis which is on the railway line from Klosters to Zurich. You may know that whilst Davos hosts the World Economic Forum each January, Klosters is a much prettier internally renowned alpine resort, famous for its UK Royal Family connections in the ski season.

On the occasion of our long run, the area had enjoyed a particularly heavy snowfall. By taking the route down to Kublis we were in virgin snow. No tracks. Pure heaven. Until, that is, our guide missed seeing the signpost to take us to the railway station in the small town. The sign post was totally buried in the deep snow. So we ended up skiing cross country, through a forest and down to the river but on the wrong side.

Finding a crossing point was troublesome. And it was getting dusk. The river was flowing strongly. Eventually, we cross and find the railway line. I suppose there are not too many places which permit travellers to flag down a train which then stops to pick us up. But eventually a Swiss train did, thankfully.

Now, alcohol and skiing are not particularly compatible. At least not if taken at the same time, on the slopes.

Skiing in Austria with a friend, we decided to take a drink at the end of a ski day just prior to skiing off the mountain and before heading back to our hotel. The mistake I made was in being persuaded to have a second jaeger tea in a very comfortable and warm alpine chalet bar in front of a roaring log fire.

Well, it was cold outside and we had had a tiring day. We knew we didn't have any more lifts to take, particularly as they were just closing for the day. Little did I realise how potent these seemingly innocuous drinks were until we came outside to put on our ski's whereupon I immediately fell down, notwithstanding my ski's were just by the chalet and left on level ground. I also noticed it had gone dark.

We had been the last to leave and didn't notice the hour was getting late. Luckily we only needed to ski about a kilometre down the mountain.

I'm afraid I was rather giggly and couldn't stand up. We finally managed to ski off. The stars were glistening on the frozen snow, lighting our way down. Certainly I had lost my technique. We did eventually reach the safety of our hotel, but I decided that never again would I mix alcohol and skiing. Definitely not to be recommended.

I subsequently discovered that the hot jaeger tea included a cocktail of Schnapps, rum and orange juice.

I can honestly say it was pretty enjoyable at the time but I am happy to report that I have never repeated this particular cocktail which could have had catastrophic consequences.

Chapter 7 Birmingham

Sheffield to Birmingham might not appear to be the most thrilling journey, but for me it turned out to be the right one after moving in 1967.

In spite of the Brummagem dialect, back then Birmingham was an exciting place to be. This is equally true today. Certainly serious misjudgements were made in the 1960's when some beautiful Victorian buildings were pulled down to make way for modern monstrosities and it became a city both made and built for motor cars, having a concrete girdle constraining the city centre and serving as its inner ring road. The mini after all was designed and made here. We might also blame the German Luftwaffe for uninvitingly rearranging the architecture and infrastructure thus forcing the process of re-planning.

Having a population of over 1 million it is certainly the engine room of the West Midlands conurbation, the second largest city in the UK and the largest local authority in Europe. Ok, much of the architecture is not particularly inspiring but take a walk down New Street or Colmore Row and glance at the upper levels to appreciate the detail of the Victorian architecture easily missed at street level.

In the last two decades or so it has had a succession of visionary leaders having the determination to undo some of the immediate post-war planning errors by re-classifying the roads and delivering world class conference and exhibition centres including Symphony Hall, home of the CBSO, the City of Birmingham Symphony Orchestra.

With three major universities it has become a city packed with young people, a digital city of science and of culture which is redefining itself subsequent to the decline of its industrial heritage developed around the industrial revolution of the 19th century. It even boasts that it has more miles of canals than Venice! If only it had its climate.

Its literary acclaim is that such writers as Samuel Johnson, Arthur Conan Doyle and JRR Tolkien had associations with the city, in addition to some notable scientists, inventors and engineers such as Matthew Boulton, Joseph Priestley and James Watt.

And who knew that both Lloyds Bank and the Midland Bank, now HSBC, were founded here in 1765 and 1836 respectively?

So much maligned, Birmingham is rich in heritage with a bright future if led strongly.

After spending a year with the wrong firm, taking me in the wrong direction, I joined a private practice firm of Chartered Surveyors called James & Lister Lea which was founded in 1846. My career blossomed. I was to become an equity partner, eventually progressing to Managing Partner and subsequently to Senior Partner, presiding over some 80 employees at its zenith, prior to merging the practice in 2001, becoming a consultant and taking partial retirement in order to pursue other interests.

This was a highly respected firm with hardworking partners and loyal staff. Having its roots in both urban and rural estate management and fine arts, as well as in architecture during the 19th century, we had a premium client base which included the Diocese of Birmingham where I was to succeed my former Senior Partner as Diocesan Surveyor following his retirement, a bishopric appointment.

Members of the Cadbury family were clients in addition to the Gooch Estate and Packington, the seat of the Earle of Aylesford. And we valued and sold the estate and contents of Sir William Lyons' home, Wappenbury Hall near Coventry shortly after his death, Sir William being the founder and designer of the Jaguar motor car.

Looking after Warwickshire County Cricket Club as well as doing some work for Aston Villa Football Club were some of my most exciting times although I was also pretty busy growing the industrial client base.

In this particular journey through my career I often fondly reflect on why our firm was looked upon with a degree of envy by some of our competitors. Our established client base was certainly from the top drawer.

Networking helped me over time to become known to many people. After all, I arrived here not knowing a single person.

Business, certainly in Birmingham, thrived on such activity where the professional and financial services sectors exchange information and contacts. Companies and business organisations are particularly good at organising events whether they be breakfasts, lunches, cocktail receptions or formal dinners. Clients and business contacts accept invitations to attend. Such events seem to be self-perpetuating. Hands are shaken, business cards exchanged and real business carried out.

I still find these fun but a great deal of stamina is an essential pre-requisite for regular attendees, particularly in the build up to Christmas.

I confess to having a particular favourite event which I always attend. A top-drawer financial services company invites its private clients and business referrers to a quality restaurant in town for its annual reception during late November. On such occasions the train for me is the essential mode of transport. Naturally both wine and food flow unreservedly.

This last November one of the host directors invited me to try the oysters. I politely declined, but then I recalled the saying:

"You needn't tell me that a man who doesn't love oysters and asparagus and good wines has got a soul, or a stomach either. He's simply got the instinct for being unhappy highly developed." - Saki (Hector Hugh Munro)

The last time I attempted to eat this delicacy was earlier in the year in Whitstable, the fishing and harbour town in North Kent. Whitstable Oysters are world famous.

I was taken to the Crab and Winkle restaurant in the Fish Market. I tried one but they are not my favourite shell food and I resorted to a plate of whelks, winkles and mussels. After all, oysters are a rare sight indeed where I was brought up close to the banks of the toxic River Don in Wincobank!

I threw caution to the wind when the director laced an iced oyster with lemon, added a drop of Tabasco sauce and offered it to me. I have to say it was delicious and more followed.

By the time I arrived home it seemed like I had the taste of the Thames Estuary in my mouth.

My professional and other voluntary work, including my non-executive roles with other companies, brought me in touch with local politicians including a succession of Leaders and Chief Executives of Birmingham City Council.

One such leader was a cigar smoker, as indeed I had become shortly after starting my career in Sheffield. I heard from a journalist that this particular Leader had been holidaying in Barbados following a meeting with Cuban embassy officials and picked up some Cohiba cigars. As he now rarely smokes he was being persuaded to auction these off. I stepped in and suggested it must first be established whether or not these were the real article. Arguably Cohiba is one of the best brands of cigars in the world but there are fakes.

"The first thing to establish," I said, "was whether or not they were genuine – after all, we are dealing with the goods of a politician!"

"We should explore their provenance." I proffered. "Vital questions a potentially interested purchaser might ask are: what is the size, colour and country of origin. For instance, whilst a Romeo Y Julieta panatela is 11.8cm long with a 34 ring gauge, a Cohiba panatela is 11.5cm with a 26 ring gauge." Not too many people know that!

"Is the colour *Double Claro, Claro, Colorado Claro, Maduro or Oscuro*? For a full-bodied and sweeter flavour I would chose a darker colour. I prefer a Colorado hue personally. They originate from Cuba but the filter is a blend of properly aged tobaccos from the Dominican Republic. And the fatter they are the slower and more smoothly they would smoke."

"It goes without saying," I exclaimed, "that it is absolutely vital to demonstrate that these cigars have been rolled on the thighs of a nubile maiden."

I felt that an inspection of the tobacco factory was essential before any bidders became too excited in the auction room. But then you would need your bank manager with you as a funding source. My suggestion seemed to kick that idea into touch!

For me a corona sized cigar sets the standard. It is Fidel Castro's favourite cigar. Is he still alive?

Anyway, the upshot of my intervention was that the planned auction sale was cancelled on the grounds that the provenance of the Leader's cigars could not be proved.

I am now looking forward to a private viewing and, with luck, testing one of them, though I'm not holding my breath!

In business, networking is an essential tool which helps to establish relationships and oil wheels. A few years ago I was invited to meet HRH Princess Anne, the Princess Royal, at a private reception sponsored by a High Street bank. Whilst waiting for her arrival in an ante-room I was asked by the then Lord Lieutenant of the West Midlands if I would be interested in succeeding him as the next Non-Executive Chairman of a local commercial radio station having a London based plc parent company.

When I responded that I knew nothing about the radio business he replied:

"You don't need to, Glyn. Just read the papers prior to attending the monthly board meetings. The station's executives will do all the work. What's more it will be fun!"

This was a 3 year term of office which I accepted with relish. It was indeed fun, though with some serious bits and contrasted with my more sedate day job as an arbitrator. Both in the studio and at lunches, dinners and parties I was to meet quite a few pop stars and bands such as Westlife and UB40 in addition to celebrity DJ's such as Chris Tarrant and Tony Blackburn.

These days I get my fix by listening every Saturday when I can to Brian Matthew's "Sounds of the 60's" on BBC Radio 2.

Chapter 8 Solihull

Before finally moving into the town of Solihull, Maggie and I bought a 200 year old farmhouse with almost a couple of acres just outside the village of Berkswell. Thanks to the boundary changes in 1974 this historic village which was in Warwickshire now forms part of the Metropolitan Borough of Solihull.

We had just enough land to accommodate two donkeys called Hector and Snout, along with Domino our first German Shepherd and a cat. Sadly Domino was to be shot because she'd slipped away into a neighbouring farmer's field with another farm dog but where sheep were grazing. She was doing no harm but the farmer, not recognising her from a distance shot her. Devastating at the time.

Our next Alsatian was stolen we think during the Cruft's Dog Show weekend at the nearby National Exhibition Centre. She was never recovered.

Hopefully our third German Shepherd, Inca, whom we bought much later and almost 20 years after we had moved into Solihull, will enjoy a longer life. She is now just over a year old and I suppose in doggie terms a teenager. She seems to have boundless energy, defying all authoritative dog training manuals but a real hit with our grandchildren.

Meanwhile, back in those Berkswell days, our two sons, Chris and Simon were attending Solihull School some 8 miles away and had to be driven there daily.

After a couple of years and a number of incidents involving the donkeys escaping into the village, we decided to relocate them onto a donkey farm in Cornwall. The final decider was when I saddled up Hector. I was just climbing ever so gently onto his back when Simon sneaked up behind us and gave him a whack on the backside, causing him, not unnaturally, to rear up promptly dislodging me unceremoniously onto my own bottom.

In any event I am pretty wary of horses at the best of times, so for me to even think about riding a donkey was an ambitious task. As it ended in abject failure, my wife arranged to send the donkeys to the Cornish sanctuary. I think much to the relief of the entire village residents.

With the help of my building surveying friend Mike and his wife Jenny we were to spend 16 years of our lives renovating this former farmhouse, before finally deciding to move closer to civilisation, into town.

All those years ago I had ignored Mike's pleadings at the auction sale in 1976 that I shouldn't touch the house with a bargepole.

Those were busy days, coinciding as they did with developing my career at the private practice firm of Chartered Surveyors which I had joined. A couple of evenings each week I began teaching the esoteric subject of valuation to part-time students at Birmingham

Polytechnic as the Birmingham City University was then known. Challenging, but satisfying. Even the students seemed to enjoy these sessions. We had a good rapport.

Then our two sons came along. What a handful! I seemed to be flying, metaphorically.

This I found was a good deal better than flying in the physical sense. One of my clients was a pilot. He persuaded me to undertake a valuation of his home and in return he would give me a flying lesson. He owned a share of a 2-seater Cessna out of Coventry Airport at Baginton.

The day looked promising: blue windless skies, frost on the ground. Visibility excellent. At least it would have been had I been able to see out of the windscreen. Seems I needed to be taller to fly this machine. Seated, with the controls at my hand, my nose barely reached the bottom of the windscreen. All my enthusiasm for flying shot out of the window. I now know what it is like to be flying blind!

We flew over our Berkswell home. Maggie was outside hanging out her washing at a pre-determined hour. We dropped naughtily below 1000 feet. The air traffic controller at Baginton snapped at us to get back up. I slid open the side window, intending to give her a wave. Not a good idea at 100mph. I very nearly lost my arm.

I soon decided flying was not for me and should anyway be left to taller humans.

Maggie and I were to become members for a while of the Cripple's Car Circle, a support group which picked up disabled people, usually from their own homes and took them on outings for the day. Most satisfying.

Then came my initiation into freemasonry. I joined a Lodge in Edgbaston and progressed inexorably through the Master's chair by 1988 after which Provincial Grand Lodge honours were conferred.

Contrary to popular belief, freemasons do not plot to overthrow governments, blow up the Houses of Parliament or act in any way which can be described as subversive. Unless they were doing these things behind my back!

Within the movement one is regularly reminded that freemasonry is neither a religion nor a substitute for religion. It seeks to inculcate in its members a standard of conduct and behaviour which it believes to be acceptable to all creeds. It is not a competitor of religion but complementary to it. Every member is required to believe in a Supreme Being, not necessarily God.

The apparent secrecy which masonry exudes is merely observed so as to enhance the experience of its initiates. Within the privacy of Lodge Rooms stories are enacted allegorically. After all, it wouldn't do to read the final chapter of a book before starting at the beginning. Wouldn't such practice negate the point of reading?

I soon realised that freemasonry did much for humanity, particularly those in need. Alas I was to resign eventually, as my interest waned and other activities took precedent.

One such interest which ran parallel for a time was the Round Table movement. Whilst I worked in Birmingham, we were still living in Berkswell. Friends living here persuaded me to join their Table in Coventry, just down the road.

Unlike most of the members of Coventry Three Spires Round Table, I was never able to drink more than a couple of pints of beer without feeling the worse for wear. Even now, some 30 years on, my antics, or really, shortcomings, are discussed around dining tables. Some friends will never allow me to forget certain experiences I had with them on a rugby trip to Paris.

Coming from good Yorkshire stock my naivety in a Parisian nightclub showed when, upon being presented with the drinking bill, I turned deathly pale, excused myself to find the toilet and promptly climbed through an open window leading onto the street at the rear of the club, giving me my first sighting of the Sacre Coeur.

My friends were left to talk their way out of this sticky situation and avoid having to settle the enormously inflated bill. By the time they reached our hotel I was fast asleep in my bed.

I recall booking Ken Dodd for one of our Round Table Gala nights. It followed the year after we had had Bob

Monkhouse as our guest after-dinner speaker, a great success. Doddy, on the other hand was a disaster. I'd booked him for 90 minutes and after some 30 minutes he'd lost the audience. At the interval I paid him his fee and suggested he might as well stop there. "No way," he shouted, "you've paid me for 90 minutes of my time and that's what you're going to get!" I squirmed, as did the hapless audience when he duly resumed his act after the break.

Somehow I managed to be appointed as our Round Table's International Relations Officer. One duty was to organise trips to like-minded international Tables such as Delft in Holland, and to Jodoigne in Belgium, where I organised twinning ceremonies and made speeches in both French and Walloon!

The Europeans do like to twin.

A classic image comes to mind of a certain senior "honorary" member of our Table, a former industrialist and hotelier, now living on the island of Guernsey, who accompanied us to Delft. After the customary bellyful of ale, we were walking along a narrow street in the centre of the town with a mixture of town houses, shops and bars on either side. A workman was working on a steeply sloping roof with his ladder precariously perched on a house wall, extending across the pavement. Well, rather than tempting fate and simply walking beneath this ladder, our honorary member decided it was better to pick up the ladder and carry on walking with it down the street.

I have no idea what the Dutch builder was shouting from the rooftop but I can't imagine it was repeatable!

I suppose I was involved in numerous adventures involving the Round Table movement. But there is one which I still recall with a smile. Round Tablers by definition are a gregarious bunch. And the European Tablers are no exception.

I had driven my wife and our sons to Hyeres next to Toulon on the French Riviera for a summer camping holiday. As holidays go this regrettably did not rank amongst the best. How was I to know that there were salt beds near the camp site, a serious breeding ground for mosquitoes? Or that at 5am each morning a couple of Super Etendard French jetfighters would take off from a nearby military base for manoeuvres and wake up the whole camp site...it was shortly after the Argentinean war of 1982 and these were the aircraft type used by the Argentinean air force carrying exocet missiles.

This evoked memories of staying in a Belgian tabler's home in Jodoigne when we heard Mrs Thatcher's announcement of the outbreak of the war with Argentina over the sovereignty of the Falkland Islands which was to last just 3 months.

It was possibly unfortunate that I had persuaded our close friends Mike and Jenny to meet up with us on this site, as they also enjoyed camping under canvas and, strangely, they did not seem to trust my judgement in subsequent years.

On this particular holiday I was wearing a cap which bore the emblem of a Belgian Round Table, Jodoigne, which my Table had twinned with. This was "spotted" and I was invited to join the Hyeres Round Table for dinner, which I duly accepted.

This proved to be another nail in my coffin.

Leaving my wife and friends behind I left the camp site in good form only to return much worse for wear and forgetting where we had pitched tent. After collapsing through the tent of a French family during the pitch black early hours of the morning and finally finding our own pitch, I was definitely not flavour of the week with a number of the campers, nor my wife and friends.

The sell-by date as a tabler was 40. It is now 45. At that age we get chucked out but only to continue our *joie de vivre* under the cloak of a club known as Fellowship After Round Table.

Don't work out the acronym!

Chapter 9 Valldemossa

I recall the Gods were somewhat propitious when we first discovered Majorca. They'd ended their wrath by sending the severe weather which devastated Southern England just before I was scheduled to fly out to the island.

I flew one Saturday in October 1987. By then the severe storms had subsided. Some 15 million trees had just been uprooted and 22 people were sadly killed. Seeing the devastation from the air was horrific.

Quite apart from these dreadful storms which had abated in time for my visit, I remember this period very well as it also coincided with Black Monday, the worst crash on the stock market around the world for many years.

Just maybe the Gods were trying to communicate with me and I didn't read the signs! In the week I was there I ended up agreeing to buy an apartment overlooking the bay in Puerto Pollensa.

We clearly decided such warnings were to be ignored and went on to enjoy holidays on this island every year since.

But it was now time to move our base. Grandchildren had come along and it became clear that we had outgrown our two-bedroomed apartment.

I first spotted the *finca,* a country house on the outskirts of the mountain village of Valldemossa, on the internet in 2002 and arranged to meet the diminutive estate agent at our place in Puerto Pollensa.

This charming lady was a middle-aged Peruvian, it seemed with little driving experience. I judged this by the battered car she was driving. Following our inspection she drove us back to our apartment. Whilst joining the motorway at Binissalem she managed to drive up the wrong lane. It was a white-knuckle ride! Upon seeing cars speeding towards us I suggested she might care to move over into the correct lane. She did, just in the nick of time!

Such is the tenuous design of Majorcan roads which, when mixed with Peruvian drivers, serves up a potentially lethal cocktail.

Earlier, whilst driving us along the narrow mountainous road following the inspection, she had managed to add a further sizeable dent in her little car, just clipping the side of a stone retaining wall put there to prevent vehicles from toppling down the 1000 foot drop to the sea. She merely shrugged and carried on driving. In spite of this sobering experience we were to complete the purchase of this house in the mountains.

My partial retirement had enabled me to set up my own practice in Solihull as a consultant and arbitrator, resolving disputes between landlords and tenants of commercial property. It was also at this stage when we decided to buy the house in Chopin's Valldemossa, in the north-western region of Majorca.

You will be hard pressed to meet many locals who speak English in this region. And why should they? Having been coming now for a few years I absolutely enjoy this area, it having forever remained natural, largely unspoilt by tourism, in spite of Chopin's overpowering influence in Valldemossa where lots of tourist shops have sprouted along its narrow cobbled streets, each seemingly vying to sell similar wares to vast numbers of visitors arriving in coach loads off the cruise ships which sail daily into the Port of Palma.

But each time I visit nothing ever really seems to change, except, perhaps, the price of a *café americano* or, these days, the cost of bread and the price of petrol.

The actor Michael Douglas financed the building of the Costa Nord cultural centre in Valldemossa in the year 2000. It was then acquired by the Balearic Government in 2004. This centre seems to be the first port of call for the tourists who are taken to the auditorium and treated to a Michael Douglas narrated film of the area and its history. It runs concerts, gastronomic evenings, a film club and guided excursions into the *Serra de Tramuntana*, the Tramuntana Mountains.

I take off my sombrero to the Costa Nord locals. They get into the part by dressing up in the traditional Majorcan costume: men in broad knee-length breeches and the women in ankle-length skirts with brightly coloured aprons with a richly embroided fringed shawl made of finest silk. During the early part of the twentieth century it was customary to dress up on Sundays in the traditional Majorcan costume, including a straw hat.

Douglas's holiday home in Valldemossa is called S'Estaca, strikingly built in a style of the Moors with whitewashed castellated walls and located on the cliffs just above the Port of Valldemossa. It was built by the Archduke Luis Salvador in the late 19th Century.

In the woods leading steeply down to the sea from a privately owned museum near us called Miramar is a path, treacherous in part before it levels and follows a contour. One of its routes passes alongside S'Estaca.

One day, I persuaded Jordi and Bernardo to show me this particular track which eventually emerges onto the narrow winding road leading down to the Port. The Douglas's were in residence, although regrettably I didn't see Catherine taking a discreet swim, thanks to the heavy fencing around the pool area. Walking by, I realised we were being followed. It was a Golden Retriever, friendly and wagging its tail. Both Jordi and Bernardo were telling it to return to the house from whence it came. Alas, to no avail. It continued to follow us.

At this point, it occurred to me that the dog might not actually understand either Majorcan or Castilian Spanish. I asked the guys to stop shouting at it whilst I established which language it understood. Sure enough, upon my command in English to sit, it did indeed sit. That cracked it. It was evident this lucky dog was owned by Catherine Zeta-Jones. So I commanded it to go back to the house. It duly did, much to the amusement of all.

Another interesting fact about Valldemossa, arguably its most famous, is that Frederick Chopin happened to stay there in the winter of 1838-1839 together with his mistress, the French writer, George Sand. They stayed in the ancient monastery known as the *"Real Cartuja de Valldemossa"*. This building was inhabited by the Carthusian monks from 1399 until 1835. The fact that the Polish pianist and composer stayed there a whole winter seems to be enough for the Department of Tourism and the *ajuntamiento*, the local authority, to dine out on this fact it seems in perpetuity, judging by the number of coaches packed with tourists visiting here daily, the whole year round.

I understand that George Sand went around Valldemossa in men's clothing. She also smoked cigars! These days we have a name for such antics!

Two of Chopin's pianos remain in the monastery. It was here that he composed many of his Preludes, in the cold wet winter of 1838/39. It was the cold, damp monastery where his health deteriorated, both physically and mentally, eventually dying of tuberculosis in 1848.

For many years in August a Chopin festival of music has been held here, in the grounds of the monastery with a good many other cultural activities also taking place.

It was the present King Juan Carlos of Spain, a regular visitor to the island with the Spanish Royal Family, who is said to have proclaimed "how I would have liked to be the Archduke who owned the road along the Valldemossa and Deià coast!" The Archduke purchased his first estate known as Miramar in 1872.

Some years ago our property was acquired out of the Miramar estate. Located just below us, it now houses a museum rather like Son Marroig just 2 km down the mountain road owned by the same family, displaying furniture, documents and works of art related to the Archduke in particular, but also to Ramon Llull who is described as Majorca's favourite son.

Born in Palma in the 13th century to the son of a wealthy noble family from Barcelona, Ramon Llull remained uneducated for the first part of his life. He became a page at the Court of King James II. Having neglected his education, he could only speak Catalan. It was finding religion that was to transform him. He became a Franciscan monk, travelled a spell then came back to Majorca, studying Arabic for nine years.

A Franciscan monastery was founded by him in nearby Miramar, where he set up a School to teach Arabic to the monks. Remember, the Moors still occupied Spain at this time. The language school at Miramar was thus founded, with the blessing of Pope John XXI. He was to become a prolific writer and poet, a philosopher and missionary. His presence is noted all over the island.

There is a cave with a window carved out of the stone, not 200 metres from our house, hidden in the mountain forest. Here he is reported to have lived in solitude for a number of years whilst undertaking his studies.

Ramon Llull has been beatified, but not yet achieved sainthood. The good Lord works in mysterious ways.

If the upper part of Valldemossa is dominated by the Carthusian monastery where Chopin and his lover spent that now famous winter, it is the lower part of the *pueblo* which houses the parish church of Sant Bartomeu, devoting itself to the life of Santa Catalina.

Catalina Thomas was born here in 1531, a bronze statue identifying her birthplace. She was to work in paid service as a maid and perform miracles in the nearby fields. She died in 1574, eventually achieving sainthood in 1930, Majorca's only saint.

Her life is celebrated annually in Valldemossa each August with religious, cultural, gastronomic and sporting events for the local inhabitants. Children dress in national costume with "La Beateta", the Blessed one, being represented by a chosen child.

Chopin, not to be outdone, gets his annual moment of deification when his own festival takes place following the homage to Santa Catalina.

At least it's all good for tourism and the local economy!

In the local bar Jordi and others are always talking about the 'good old days'. This is a reference to when Franco was in power, when the Spanish were required to speak only the national language, Castilian Spanish, the other languages such as Catalan were banned. And the peseta was the unit of currency. Of course, the dictator ruled from 1939 until his relatively recent death in 1975, thus memories are still vivid.

The island of Majorca was, in effect, considered wealthy, and thus the islanders were broadly in favour of this dictator. It was generally the poor and the left wingers who joined the Republican forces fighting against Franco's right wing Nationalists. The Republican strongholds of *Catalonia*, centred in Barcelona, and the *Pais Vasco*, the Basque region, fought fiercely against *el Generalisimo* until they were finally overwhelmed. The city of Barcelona was captured by the Nationalist forces in January, 1939, opening the way for Franco to march into Madrid, bringing to an end the bloody Spanish Civil War which started in 1936.

Franco's burial place is in the mountains an hour's drive northwest of Madrid, dominated by a 150 metre high crucifix. It's known as the *Valle de los Caidos*, the Valley of the Fallen. Just now the Spanish government are about to take a decision as to its future. The real problem is the very thought of having a monument to a tyrannical dictator where extremists still gather annually to mark the anniversary of his death. Unfortunately there also are the remains of some 12,000 soldiers from the defeated Republican side in the war, who were buried alongside the Franco supporters at the valley without families' knowledge or permission.

It was Franco who named Prince Juan Carlos as the next Head of State. He was designated king in 1975 according to Franco's Law of Succession. King Juan Carlos I then proceeded to successfully oversee the transition of Spain from dictatorship to a parliamentary democracy having survived a major military coup which was attempted in conjunction with the Guardia Civil in 1981.

The King does seem to be widely popular, though I suspect not entirely by all his subjects throughout Catalonia and certain other Spanish regions that are still fighting for greater independence and the protection of their own individual language.

He, his wife Queen Sofia and the rest of the Spanish Royal Family spend a good part of each summer on the island of Majorca. They stay in the Marivent Palace in the capital, Palma, with the imposing and historic Almudaina Palace, opposite the Cathedral, being his official office, used for state functions and ceremonies such as the changing of the Guard on the last Saturday of each month.

Interestingly, unlike the UK monarchy, they can often be spotted dining in the local restaurants and browsing in the shops. They will even visit such tourist attractions as Valldemossa.

The family seems to be everyone's idea of what archetypal monarchs mean for the people. Even the press is reverential towards them, but here in Spain the media does have a greater degree of restriction placed upon it than is the case with the UK media. And perhaps strangely I personally find that acceptable.

But even today, the Guardia Civil are both feared and respected by the locals.

They often take coffee in my usual bar in Valldemossa.

I tend to know when they are about. After buying our daily bread we visit the local bar. I always end up buying Jordi his "*cortado*", a milky expresso which he drinks in one sip while I take ages enjoying my *americano*. Suddenly Jordi lowers his voice. I look furtively behind me and see the policemen in their green uniforms overtly carrying pistols.

Somewhat worryingly but possibly understandably no-one seems to befriend them, unlike the friendlier local *policia municipal* clad in blue with whom Jordi and I chat and even occasionally take coffee with them. In any event I like to acknowledge the local police as I need their advice and help sometimes.

Continuing in a furtive and conspiratorial manner, Jordi leans closer to me, placing his forefinger on his nose, extended upwards beyond one eye, touching his forehead and speaks in whispers if we are talking about 'the good old days' or the monarchy even. I am never sure whether he is guarding his comments against the keen ears of the Guardia Civil or perhaps equally against the ears of those breakfasting in the bar, some of whom possibly being Republican sympathisers!

This is clearly a throwback to allegations of numerous instances of police brutality under Franco, notwithstanding that the Guardia Civil was originally founded as a national police force in 1844 under a monarchy.

For certain, the nerves are still raw at the edges regarding this aspect of recent Spanish history.

One afternoon in the summer of 2009, I was driving towards Palma Nova, with my wife and two grandchildren, when there was much police activity just as we were entering the resort. We were stopped by the Guardia Civil and redirected away from the town. The weather was blisteringly hot and we were going nowhere fast. Huge traffic jams suddenly occurred. What should have only taken 30 minutes to return to Valldemossa took some two and a half hours.

We later discovered that a bomb had been placed underneath a police patrol car parked in front of a Guardia Civil station in Palma Nova, close to where we were driving. Two Guardia Civil officers were killed. It was the first deadly terrorist attack in the Balearic Island, believed top be the work of ETA terrorists.

At 8.30am the following morning, Jordi and I were travelling along the winding and at that time desolated road towards Valldemossa for our daily bread and caffeine intake when suddenly out from nowhere an armed Guardia Civil officer, arm threateningly outstretched, stepped into the middle of the narrow road, requiring us to stop.

Jordi, ever the hero, looked more terrified than me. I was driving a fairly battered hired car, with Spanish plates. Two other policemen, with guns, also stepped into the road. Clearly they were searching for the terrorists, believing that they might just possibly be making their way by foot over the mountains and down to the secluded and largely inaccessible Port de Valldemossa, famous for its smuggling opportunities and for landing illegals.

I have to admit I was a little beside myself when the first officer halted our car and stood menacingly feet astride, hand on his opened pistol holster staring intently at me. The other two guys came to each side of the car, demanding that we wind down the windows.

"*Buenos dias.*" I uttered, trying to sound very English, which with my accent was not difficult.

"*Bon dia!*" said Jordi to the other, looking and definitely sounding like a Majorcan, which, judging by the country's history, might have been a mistake.

Jordie instantly became subservient. This, to our mutual relief, seemed to satisfy the two officers, who, having peered into the car, decided we were not a danger to anyone and sent us on our way.

A sticky moment and one we still talk about.

Today it is the constant arrival and capture of illegal immigrants off the island's remote extremities which occupy greatly the Guardia Civil. A special radar facility has been installed across the southern part of the Balearics to better control and detect nefarious maritime activities, which mainly consist of small boats attempting to land illegally.

Spain has a national holiday which doubles with the honouring of the patroness of the Guardia Civil. It is known as "*Doce de Octubre*", 12th October. This is what we would describe as a bank holiday, but it is taken as an opportunity to celebrate the armed forces and the Civil Guard. Originally it was known as Columbus Day to commemorate the discovery of America by Christopher Columbus.

It is clear there is much ignorance as to the motive of such celebrations which take place on this day throughout the country, which include a military parade in Madrid presided over by King Juan Carlos and Queen Sofia. This to an outsider might appear to be somewhat paradoxical. We remember that the Guardia Civil were the enforcers of the Franco dictatorship and party to the attempted 1981 coup but the custom is continued by a democracy.

I suppose it is one way of forging closer ties with the autonomous regions Spain is known for, integrating these with the State.

As one editor of a national daily recently wrote when analysing Spain's National Day: "*Es un dia para celebrar quienes somos.*" "It is a day in celebration of who we are."

It is to Spain's credit that such celebrations do not appear divisive, at least overtly, but serve to show off to its nationals the importance of the acceptance of diversity.

Spain is indeed a diverse and, in my view, a complex country. Sadly today it has a level of unemployment more than double that of ours in the UK. Along with having a high proportion of its young people out of work, the country, as presently is the case with much of the northern hemisphere, faces an austere economic future pending a satisfactory solution eventually being found in respect of the whole of the ailing eurozone.

Their national football team are currently world champions and their tennis team including Rafa have just won the Davis Cup – again! Deservedly so. The country has a wealth of talented sportsmen.

Jordi is not sure about this, as our conversation turns to soccer.

He curtly says the majority of the team is made up of players from Barcelona FC. This I detected was a case of having sour grapes, he being ostensibly anti-Catalan and an overt supporter of Real Madrid!

In Valldemossa opinion does seem divided as to the superiority of these two clubs, either of which being well capable of more than matching in quality any of our top English clubs. The local team, Real Mallorca, whilst being also in the top Spanish league, surprisingly do not receive much attention, at least not in our bar.

Deià

Chapter 10 Deià

The north-western coastal village of Deià, close to Valldemossa, has towering limestone mountains as its backdrop. On top of a smaller hill in the centre lies the ancient church of St John the Baptist dominating the scene, strikingly illuminated at night by soft lighting.

In this area its fertile soil, supported by extensively irrigated terracing, encouraged an ideal place to settle, with some stunning vistas across the sea, the olive groves giving the village a silver green tint contrasting with the mellow hue of the honey stone-built houses clustered together on the steep hillsides.

The many orange, fig and lemon trees adorn the village, sheltered from the northerly winds and adding to the exceptional natural beauty of this popular tourist location. A half-hour steep walk leads down to the pebbled fishermans' cove, also accessed by car. An old fisherman's coastal path leads to the hamlet of Lluc Alcari and along to Port Soller, arguably offering the most attractive views on the island.

Interestingly the name Deià comes from the Arabic *ad daia* which broadly means "village".

From the early 20th century it became a haven for writers, artists and musicians. Earlier it had prospered from the production of olive oil, a major part of Majorca's economy, and now a water bottling plant provides some local employment which must have been greatly overtaken since the rapid expansion of the village from the 1970's with its numerous bars and restaurants.

The village cemetery adjoins the church. In one corner, easily missed, is a simple gravestone marked *Poeta*, poet, which identifies the grave of the English writer and poet Robert Graves who wrote "I Claudius". Living in Deià much of his work was both written and published in his home called Ca N'Alluny, on the edge of the village.

On occasion he was visited by such Hollywood celebrities as Ava Gardner, Alec Guinness and Peter Ustinov. He died in 1985 aged 90, his house recently having been converted into a museum by his family who still live in Deià.

I was to stay a weekend at what was then Richard Branson's five star hotel, La Residencia, in Deià, when searching for a house in the Tramuntana mountains. They had 2 tennis courts ran I discovered, by Shayne, the professional coach, who hails from Australia. I stayed in touch with Shayne, who asked me to come to social tennis on Sundays when I'm on the island. Well, needless to say I take up this opportunity whenever possible. I find myself playing against both local residents of varying nationalities and guests staying in the hotel.

Recently, I was on the island for 3 weeks. Shayne phoned. A hotel guest was looking for someone to play singles against daily, during his fortnight's stay.

It transpired that the guest was there with his 85 year old mother, enjoying a holiday which was costing €10,600 for his mother's room and €7,400 for his, bed and breakfast only. Lunches were taken by the tranquil pool side and costing some €38, with evening dinner for two usually costing him around €240 for a 3 course meal including a glass of wine, bottled water and coffee.

Naturally we rounded off our tennis matches with a glass of cold San Miguel either on their beautiful Hibiscus-bordered terraces interspersed with gnarled olive and carob trees, looking out over the attractive village or enjoying the tranquillity of the pool-side bar.

Not for the faint-hearted the cost of dining out in Deià. Thanks to the well-heeled guests of the hotel looking for a variety of gourmet meals the local restaurants have been quick to spot such a God-sent opportunity. They now pander to the tourists' needs and of course at a commensurate cost.

In fact we've dined at most of the restaurants in Deià or taken *tapas* and beer at a local bar, Xelini's, where, on occasion, diners could well find themselves either in close company of Andrew Lloyd Webber and his family who own a house or two in the village or some other celebrity staying at La Residencia..

The word *"tapas"* is a collective noun for small plates of savouries, the word originating from the Spanish *tapa*, lid. The custom is said to have started by inn-keepers placing a slice of bread over the customer's wine glass to keep out flies and dust between sips. The Andalucians then developed the idea by balancing a morsel of something tasty on top of the bread. There are now many varieties of this uniquely Spanish experience, taken as a snack at all times of the day.

Since 1988 our Puerto Pollensa apartment had become our bolthole; our escape from the prolific pace of life we were experiencing in Birmingham. The house we were to buy much later in Valldemossa began to suit us better in later life. More tranquil, with only wild mountain goats for company, though Jordi was never far away! Both could be a real handful.

Incidentally were you to holiday in Puerto Pollensa you would need to buy your supplies of Faustino VII *rosado* wine and Gordon's Gin pretty smartly. We have a Scottish friend, Alister, who, with his wife Delma, spends 6 months in residence near the old town of Pollensa. This larger than life dour Scotsman is no respecter of other people's drinking needs. Upon arrival he visits the main supermarkets in town and buys up every bottle of Faustino VII and Gordon's he can lay his hands on. His thirst for these labels is insatiable.

At numerous lunches and dinners in his company I've long since been under the table whilst Alister is merely getting into full swing. It tends to be the Magno, a Spanish brandy which does it for me. I can never say no, much to my wife's chagrin.

On a recent occasion after a rather long lunch in a local restaurant, the brandy came out. I noticed the different label, Alma de Magno. It was somewhat expensive.

"I've never seen you drink that particular brand!" I exclaimed.

"No, I have a bottle at home but I've never served it to you!" he said, smiling.

He was on good form that day. I mentioned that my hired car was an Opel Corsa and it seemed underpowered. "Yes", he said, "it is called a Vauxhall Nova in the UK but they can't call it a Nova here in Spain". I twigged that the name *Nova* in Spanish translates to "it doesn't go!"

On one particular occasion after dining with Alister when I was staying alone on the island I very nearly missed my plane. I felt so ill upon being driven to Palma airport that to this day I've no idea how I found my way home on landing in Birmingham. Of course I'm much wiser now. I always ensure I take a couple of Paracetamol before meeting my friend followed by a couple afterwards. Essential preparation to avoid those terrible hangovers, abstinence not being an option!

After my tennis opponent from the hotel had whetted my appetite by telling me what he'd been having for his rather pricey dinner, I was able to contrast this with dinner I'd just had. My wife had not yet joined me on the island. She was due to fly from Birmingham some 6 days after me. Well I needed to think about dinner a few days into my arriving. Jordi came to my rescue. Every Friday evening during the summer a few members of the Patanca Club of Deià meet for a friendly game.

"Would I like to join him?" he asked.

After he told me there was a cooked meal laid on after the game but it would cost me €6 I tried not to accept too quickly. Little did I realise I would be enlisted to play with Jordi's son Pedro against Jordi and his team partner Alberto. To my surprise we won, and Jordi was a little subdued during the meal, getting much ribbing from the other players.

But I digest. I really want to contrast the €240 meal (albeit for two) with my €6 meal. Pedro looks after a small estate in Soller where the owner keeps a few sheep and a large orchard. At the appropriate time Jordi will help his son slaughter the lambs and prepare them for the freezer. To show his gratitude the owner presents a couple of lambs to Pedro, who promptly brings one along to the Petanca Club.

During the match the *cordero,* lamb, had been cooking slowly with herbs and wine, before being introduced into a large paella-type dish where *patatas fritas* (what else!), more herbs, garlic, red wine and green beans were added. Following two delicious helpings we were then served with cream cake and coffee. Bottles of Navarra wine were put on the table, along with Majorcan green olives. All for €6 a head. And any other drinks we wanted were each priced at just €1.

I'm thinking of joining the Club!

Living in the mountains as we do when we are on the island, we feel the urge to come down to civilisation just occasionally. Quite where we head for depends on our length of stay and whether or not the grandkids are staying with us. The children still enjoy spending much of their time either splashing about in our pool or strolling with me in the mountains, mainly to track the wild goats. But they naturally also enjoy a trip to a waterpark, adventure playground or a beach.

The sandy bays of Palma Nova and Magalluf are visited as these resorts tend to be where many of the island's facilities are found. We have discovered a pleasant beach bar offering afternoon tea and jam and cream scones for just €2.75. Hardly Majorcan, but welcome nonetheless. This plus the beach sights of Magalluf are a welcome treat in the late afternoon. It certainly makes a change from stalking goats!

We discovered a wonderful quiet cove beyond the pine forest near Magalluf called Portals Vells. The beach is a little difficult to access and is frequented largely by the Spanish. Here the kids can play safely on the beach while we take a cold San Miguel in the only restaurant with an open terrace giving onto the sandy bay. There we arranged a front-line table where we ordered a late lunch of their speciality, seafood *paella* with our Majorcan friends Jose Luis and Sandra a few days before their wedding.

Jose Luis introduced our grandson Jack to one of the guests who happened to be dining with his family. It was the talented Paraguyan international professional footballer Valdez who was visiting the island to arrange a possible transfer to a Spanish *primera liga* team. His son aged 4 started kicking a ball around with Jack, it having been duly autographed by the number ten striker.

A terrific afternoon, though we are always glad to make it back up into the greater tranquillity and bliss of the mountains midway between Valldemossa and Deià.

Chapter 11 Arbitration

"I swear by Almighty God that the evidence I shall give shall be the truth, the whole truth and nothing but the truth."

Of course, it's not all play. As an experienced arbitrator involved with commercial property disputes, usually between landlord and tenants, I do receive personal appointments to act as the dispute resolver. My particular specialism is in settling rent review disputes relating to City centre office buildings, business parks and factories.

Many such disputes are settled amicably between the parties, without the necessity of the arbitrator's intervention. Some cases do, however, go live, when the arbitrator is called upon to hear the parties' differences and make an award, usually reasoned and in writing, occasionally following a formal hearing. On these occasions, all evidence is either taken on oath or affirmed.

The arbitrator is, in effect, the judge, acting in a judiciary capacity, working within the constraints laid down by statute. But he doesn't get to wear a red robe and wig – at least not yet!

Whilst it is true that the arbitrator's role is largely protected, he can nevertheless be challenged by the parties as to his own jurisdiction in any particular dispute he is to resolve. I have found this happens rarely but when it does he will need to know the appropriate law in this area and, happily and only then if it's appropriate, may decide his own jurisdiction without the necessity of the parties taking this off to court.

My training in this fascinating area is updated twice yearly at focused day conferences, when like minded arbitrators get together to receive legal updates and exchange experiences.

Recently, I had to decide an interesting case. I ran an oral hearing. The parties, or at least their advisors, appear before the arbitrator to argue their case and be cross-examined. Similar to a court of law but in an office or hotel conference room. Unlike in a law court the proceedings are in private.

The case revolved around a dispute on what was considered to be the open market annual rental value as at the relevant review date. That is, the rent which should be paid by the occupier to the landlord.

The subject unit was a large office building located in an industrial suburb of Birmingham. The lease provision, however, directed the parties to make the assumption, if not the fact, when arriving at the rental value, that the premises were located in the best area for offices in Birmingham City Centre.

As the case progressed a preliminary legal issue arose as to the length of the lease which had to be assumed from a reading or interpretation of the lease provisions. This was dealt with by a preliminary meeting held in my office and needed to be decided before the oral hearing could continue.

The outcome, i.e. what I decided, following my listening to evidence put forward by lawyers acting for each party, was to hugely impact on rental values to be adopted. Procedural matters needed also to be decided between the parties and the arbitrator, to determine how the oral hearing was to proceed. Even before that I received pleadings as to whether it was relevant to have a hearing or merely to receive written evidence from the parties.

At the appointed hour when the hearing was due to start, the parties assembled at work stations carefully separated on each side of the room.

These included the two Queen's Counsel, the parties' Lawyers and the experts who would be giving evidence. I allowed observers in the room, but not before making it quite clear that they were exactly that, observers, not participants, making them sit at the back and ensuring they were quiet at all times during the proceedings. The parties' expert witnesses were to present their respective cases and then be cross examined then re examined. I would step in with my own questions, as necessary.

Some arbitrators will record then have transcribed every word spoken. I usually don't, preferring to take notes in long-hand. The hearing was to last two days, after which I then inspected the subject property. My decision would follow shortly thereafter, in the form of a written Award, stating reasons for arriving at my decision on rental value.

Had I been practising in Spain during the 1930's I imagine I would have been a "Franquista", ruling with an iron hand; or 200 years earlier in England taking every opportunity to deport recalcitrant landlords and tenants to the colonies!

Or better still sending unscrupulous bankers to the gallows.

Thankfully for the parties no such power has been passed down to arbitrators, at least that I know of.

Happily, in this area of my work, I do get to decide who should pay costs, or in what proportion they should pay. The relevant party is required to pay me whatever is reasonably due, prior to my releasing the Award. This aspect of procedure is very reassuring to arbitrators. Should either partly feel aggrieved on any issue, they may be able to demonstrate grounds for an appeal before the courts within a specified period of time following the publication of the Award.

Whilst my work as a chartered surveyor is varied, it is this particular aspect I prefer. In arriving at this conclusion it could just probably be due to the fact that I get to be called "sir" by the protagonists including the highly qualified barristers. I mention this to my wife from time to time, but curiously it seems to fall on deaf ears!

As my decisions impact on capital values and are thus relevant to the value of the landlord's investment, I take seriously the responsibility which falls on my shoulder when invited to act as arbitrator.

All of which is a far cry from my first week at work after qualifying. The mid 1960's was swinging. The economy was buoyant and jobs were plentiful. I joined a firm of Chartered Surveyors in Sheffield earning the grand sum of £13 per week.

I remember being asked to assist in the property valuation of the famous manufacturer Viners of Sheffield, known throughout the world as the maker of high quality cutlery. At that time, steel was still being made in Sheffield. We had to measure the entire factory and prepare a plan. I was sent to measure the ladies toilets.

The "buffer girls" as they were called, who put the shine on the newly pressed cutlery and in consequence were always dirty from head to toe, got wind of this, deciding to step inside their toilet where I was in process of measuring. They locked the door and succeeded in frightening me to death.

As a joke, and they succeeded. My very first week of full time employment!

The 1965 Finance Act, which introduced capital gains tax for the first time, was to create much work for property valuers. It caused all businesses to value their capital assets.

Because of my father's engineering background I was particularly interested when I was asked to survey many iron and steelworks which then existed along Attercliffe Common, quite close to where I used to live.

Steel rolling mills were particularly hazardous to measure. I was sent to measure the Neepsend Rolling Mills for both capital gains tax purposes and for launching a challenge as to the correctness of the company's rating assessment. Whilst trying to check diagonal measurements I vividly remember jumping over red hot steel bars. These were continually being drawn out of the foundry by workers, bare-chested, sporting dirty handkerchiefs around their necks, clutching iron tongs. They would swiftly flick them across steel plated floors to where they would be stacked for cooling prior to being cut to size. Steel measuring tapes rather than linen ones were an essential item for surveyors!

No worries about health and safety issues in those days!

Shortly after becoming a partner in the Birmingham practice I was asked to give valuation advice of a kind of night club in Aston, adjoining the Aston Villa FC ground.

It was about lunchtime when I arrived. The windows were blackened and the lights were turned down low inside the club. People were dancing. I noticed a rack of ladies dresses along one side which puzzled me. The penny dropped when it became clear that all the customers were men.

I was conducting the inspection on my own, intending to measure the premises using a 5ft measuring rod which I take with me everywhere. I aborted the task and beat a hasty retreat back to the office. I am sorry to disclose that I sent two graduates to the club, suggesting they take with them a tape measure rather than a 5ft measuring rod!

My present role as an arbitrator has to show transparency and lack of bias towards a party to the dispute. Moreover I have to demonstrate that I have no conflict or involvement with the property, a nearby property or a party to the dispute which has existed over the last 5 years and which should be disclosed or should lead me to decline the appointment.

An arbitrator, as well as demonstrating professional knowledge, has to have an understanding of the appropriate statute and case law in addition to adopting the rules of natural justice. We can be and indeed are challenged, albeit rarely, on our own jurisdiction to hear a case. Cases may proceed *ex parte* and these days one party might easily go into receivership.

There is a panoply of issues including the considering of directions to be given regarding the disclosure of relevant documents which may need to be decided by an arbitrator as well as the settling of any preliminary legal issues prior to determining the substantive issue in dispute.

All practising RICS arbitrators are required to be reassessed by an RICS President's panel every 5 years as being competent in this position. Such practice which has evolved in recent years is of major comfort to the users of the service. And keeps all practising arbitrators on their toes!

Continual training is thus paramount as current practice and case law develop.

In Birmingham last year I was asked to chair the bi-monthly meetings of the Arbitration Club of the West Midlands branch of the Institute of Arbitrators. This was great fun but with a serious side which challenges the grey matter. I am presently preparing a series of talks on arbitrations which I have been asked to present to recently qualified graduates of the other professional body of which I am a member, the Royal Institution of Chartered Surveyors.

Being an arbitrator is indeed a challenging but hugely rewarding role both in the mental as well as, occasionally I am glad to say, in the material sense.

But I can't help thinking we should be donning red gowns and grey wigs to help us in our deliberations! As for introducing deportations...

Chapter 12 Wedding in the Sun

"*Policia, policia*!" I heard the laboured footsteps of my helper Jordi as he negotiated the remaining dozen stone steps leading onto our terrace.

The cry "*policia*" is yet another of the adopted Majorcan's practical jokes, a reference to the day the two policemen arrived at our *finca* to investigate a plume of smoke emanating from our land.

The incident happened one June when I visited the island, a few days ahead of my wife. I decided to have a pig roast, or, at least, I asked Jordi if he would light our outside oven, fuelled with pine, holm oak and olive firewood and prepare a small pig for roasting. Outside wood fired ovens, each being fondly known as an "*horno mallorquin*", are found dotted all over rural Majorca, adjoining the old farmhouses, generally built from the local stone.

His reputation for cooking roast suckling pig is legendary, at least between Soller and Valldemossa. It is yet another speciality of the island. He had bought on my behalf all the necessary accoutrements for cooking the piglet – a decent bottle of Spanish brandy (Fundador or 301 was definitely a no go), herbs, a *crianza* red wine and lots of lemons from his orchard. The process takes about 4 hours. So the oven was lit at

08.30 when Jordi then returned to his *casita* to prepare the feast.

Jordi had invited his friends to our place for 1pm precisely, to sample at my expense, the roast suckling pig with *patatas fritas* of course!

Well, my stone built oven, alongside the elaborate stone barbecue, had not been lit for some considerable time. It had been smoking for about an hour when I heard shouts of "*Policia, senor.*" Through the dry summer period the island has a yellow and orange spotter plane whose principal function is to identify potential fires and alert the local police in the particular region. So it was that I'd been spotted by this plane. Hence the visit.

The policemen were actually friendly, General Franco having long since gone. Once they had satisfied themselves that I was not about to cause a forest fire they simply required me to put on hand a hosepipe before they promptly returned to Deià.

Rightly so, it is necessary to first obtain permission from the local authority prior to lighting a fire, especially in the summer when garden bonfires are banned outright. Jordi calls 112, the equivalent of our 999, announces his name simply as Jordi of Valldemossa, and alerts the authorities that he's about to light an outside oven. Of course he is well known to them and due process has been satisfied.

Out of this experience, the idea was born that we might hold our own fiesta at our place, *Casa de S'Eura*, following the announcement that our eldest son Chris was to marry Alison on the 24th October 2004 in the quaint old church of *San Juan el Baptista* on the hill overlooking picturesque Deià, just 5 kilometres from our *casa*.

Some 72 guests arrived from the UK one blisteringly hot weekend that October, sprinkled with a few Spanish friends, to witness the ceremony.

This particular *fin de semana*, weekend, was to be indelibly etched into my memory.

Preparations started much earlier, of course. I was tasked to select the wines, both for the wedding reception and the following day's celebratory fiesta up at ours.

This was getting serious. So I enlisted our wine buff friends, Mike the doctor and his wife Bojana to help. They happened to be staying with us for their summer holiday. I had previously mentioned to them back in England that I had a most important duty for them both to carry out. Once I disclosed the task they booked their Majorcan flights that same day!

I still have our wine tasting notes. Needless to say, we must have gone through most of the wines and cavas of Spain - colour, nose, taste - awarding an overall mark out of 10. What a hardship that was! And done with aplomb, surprisingly.

Spain happens to be the third largest wine producing country in the world, after France and Italy. So every day we were pretty merry! No surprise there. The quality of wines, both from the island of Majorca and the Spanish mainland has improved immeasurably over the last 20 years.

A decision was finally taken. We all agreed, including the happy couple Chris and Alison along with Ali's parents Andy and Gilly. On the wedding day the selected *cava*, the Spanish equivalent of champagne, was to be Anna de Codorniu, *brut reserva*, whilst the *vino tinto*, red wine, was the Coto de Imaz *reserva*, 1999 from Rioja. Marques de Riscal, *rosado reserva* 2000 was the winning pink wine.

But Mike and I had other ideas. We wanted a bit of fun! We knew of a bodega in Binissalem where we could order carafes of local red wine for the following day's pig roast. We'd been drinking this over the last couple of summers. At only 5 euros for each 4 litre carafe the Yorkshire in us both decided this was too good an opportunity to miss. And it would provide an authentic touch to the occasion. In any event the reds of Binissalem are the best known on the island.

Majorca is also famous for two other drinks which I would recommend trying. As a '*digestivo*' after a heavy meal, put a few cubes of ice into a glass and add a good tot of 'Herbes de Mallorca'. This is made from some of the many wild herbs found in the Tramuntana mountains and can be in bottles of *dulce*, ie.sweet, *seco*,dry or *mesclades*, mixed. The other drink is, in my view, the best brandy produced in Spain called 'Suau' which is made locally on the island, in Marratxi.

Back to the wedding day. I agreed a corkage fee with the Food and Beverage manager of the Hotel La Residencia, who would be responsible for chilling the wine and the *cava* some 24 hours prior to opening.

The church ceremony was memorable, though we were all feeling the 32 degrees centigrade of heat that afternoon, dressed up to the nines in dark morning suits or summery dresses and hats.

For me, my enduring memory was of the Robert Graves poem I was asked to recite during the service. I considered it to be entirely apposite and moving. It is called "Symptoms of Love":

Love is a universal migraine,
A bright stain on the vision
Blotting out reason
Symptoms of true love
Are leanness, jealousy,
Laggard dawns;
Are omens and nightmares
Listening for a knock,
Waiting for a sign.
For a touch of her fingers
In a darkened room,
For a searching look.
Take courage, lover!
Could you endure such grief
At any hands but hers?

I managed to get through this from the pulpit, though I admit my eyes glazed over.

Andy and Gilly, Alison's parents, must have been immensely proud of their only daughter on that very special day.

The wedding breakfast was held at "La Residencia" hotel.

Guests were gathering on the impeccably manicured lawn, seeking welcome shade from the many parasols and palms positioned around the gardens. A talented Spanish guitarist we had discovered busking on the streets of Palma strummed hauntingly classical melodies including the evergreen "*Recuerdos de la Alhambra*", "Memories of the Alhambra".

Later as night fell and the band appeared, the happy couple finally took to the floor and danced the night away to the strains of Nat King Cole's "Let there be Love".

Fireworks eventually followed, finally bringing the party to a close.

The celebrations were to continue the following day up at ours, the expansive sea and mountains providing a romantic backdrop.

As a wedding gift, celebrity chef Jordi generously offered his services at the *fiesta* being held on our terrace suitably adorned for this special occasion. He was to prepare five pigs to be slowly roasted using both his and our *horno mallorquin,* the outside wood-fired ovens. Such a simple feast, served with *patatas fritas,* small chopped up potato cubes fried in olive oil, with *ensalada mixta* proved to be memorable.

For dessert, Jordi and his wife Polita served *ensaimada del angel*, a sweet pastry stuffed with locally grown pumpkin and a *tarta d'almendra*, an almond cake, another local speciality often served with almond ice cream.

This was washed down with carafes of local red wine which had been sourced from a bodega in nearby Binissalem, and a *rosado* wine from Rioja.

Responsibility for cooling the *San Miguels* and soft drinks was handed to Nick, one of our in-house guests. His calculation of the *cubitos de hielo*, or ice cubes, needed for this relatively simple task one might have thought, went awry. That morning he persuaded me to fill our hired car with bags of the stuff from the local *gasolinera*, petrol station. Had we crashed the vehicle into the sea it would certainly have floated. Such was the extent of his miscalculation! His defence might be that he is a lawyer so I should have twigged that he would grossly over-estimate the quantity needed!

Much later, Jordi was to serve his *coca mallorquina*, a savoury of chopped red peppers, tomatoes and onions on a flat pizza-type base cooked on the dying embers of the *horno*. Simply delicious when eaten freshly cooked and still warm.

A locally based Argentinian musician was to entertain the invitees with his Spanish guitar, adding greatly to the atmosphere.

Inevitably the party degenerated with much impromptu singing and dancing under a clear night sky, the moon and the myriad of stars illuminating the sea well below us.

An enduring magical moment added to the occasion when everyone called upon my wife's brother, Chris Spedding, to "borrow" the Spanish guitar and play us well into the night.

This was truly unforgettable, particularly when at some point both Chris and the Argentinian were both playing the one guitar at the same time. That must have been a first.

Chapter 13 A Kid with 3 Legs

It's not just the roast suckling pig or a good lamb roast which the Majorcans like. Goats, or, more accurately, wild mountain goats, are often served up. And then only the young ones.

The island has been overrun with mountain goats for many years. The government is slow to encourage their culling, so it is left to the locals living in the countryside, to nip out with their rifle and bag themselves a young wild goat. Like all animals the youngsters are the most succulent. Certainly the larger goats, probably over 9 months old, are lucky enough to escape this impromptu cull. The meat is not considered tender enough and to shoot an older goat and not to be able to enjoy eating its meat is considered to be taboo. It's just not done, unless the cull is official, when the hunters dispose of the carcasses which are not required for human consumption.

Every day around our home near Valldemossa we see and hear these creatures. We chase them away regularly in an attempt to stop them from eating our young orange, lemon and fig trees. They wreck all young trees by eating the bark and can munch their way through most young shrubs and flowers.

So, enough is enough. All is fair in love and war against these wild animals. I wouldn't mind them at all if they would only agree to respect boundaries – that is to say, they stay outside of our land, bounded by heavy pines, olive trees, and 2m high barbed wire fencing. But respecters of human boundaries they are not. So they must expect the consequences, mustn't they?

I give you this background so that you can understand the desperation which drives me to want to see the back of any wild mountain goat when the opportunity occurs.

Occasionally the Estate decides it is time to stop the continual destruction of their own young trees and flower borders around their museum, Miramar, which is open daily for visiting tourists. A couple of the Estate workers came up one morning to set a trap. Happily two of the older goats were caught and were promptly removed.

Jack decided they had been taken away to be re-trained to eat grass rather than the Estate's flowers. I hadn't the heart to disillusion him!

As budding great white hunters, the grandkids have devised a system of hand signals largely copied from Hollywood Vietnam War films and SAS sorties into the enemy jungle. Except they do get confused, forget not to shout and thus alert the enemy – the wild mountain goats, *cabras monteses*, as they are called.

On our latest summer holiday we were on a mission to spot a 3-legged goat. Well, whoever heard of a wild mountain goat having only three legs? Earlier we had been tipped off by our daughter-in-law Alison and her husband Chris who were staying in our place, holidaying before Alison had to face up to a major op back home. She text me a message saying that she had seen a 3-legged goat grazing on acorns and bark from the numerous varieties of trees surrounding us, many in our garden. I told her in no uncertain terms that I was not falling for that one. After all, any goat with only three legs would topple over, wouldn't it? So I told Alison that she should concentrate on drinking her G & T and not to try pulling my leg. Excuse the pun.

Until, that is, my grandson Jack by now aged 7 came running up to me shortly after we had arrived for our family summer holiday. He said rather excitedly that he had just seen a 3-legged goat. Maybe, I thought, in his case it couldn't have been the G & T.

Sure enough we came upon this poor creature not 20 metres away from our boundary. It seemed to be happily grazing away with not a care in the world. Its mother was also keeping a watchful eye nearby, no doubt for disbelievers like me. Luckily I was carrying my Blackberry so I quickly videoed the improbable scene as evidence for any other disbelievers.

At that moment, a Birmingham friend text me about meeting up when I came back to civilisation. A good opportunity, I thought, to apprise him of this discovery.

"Pull the other one!" he said. Clearly he was also a disbeliever, suggesting I eased back on the G & T. He even had the audacity to say that it may have only two legs by the time I'd finished my drink!

Jordi was more understanding. Surprisingly so, as this is not one of his usual traits. Whilst he admitted that he had never seen a 3-legged goat, he didn't seem phased. I imagined he would think I was joking, but took the news matter-of-factly, seemingly unperturbed by the discovery. Until that is, he finally spotted it when Jack started shouting that it had reappeared. Well, this is yet another first - the sight of Jordi actually running down our steps into the parking area where half a dozen wild goats had gathered, ready, I suspected, to reap further havoc to our young fruit trees.

As a means of attempting to cull some of these destructive creatures, someone on the estate, I suspected, had created a more permanent trap to facilitate capture.

I had seen how this had worked during a previous visit. An unsuspecting goat would be herded into a metre-wide strip of land running between the flank wall of an abandoned *casita* and the estate's boundary fence. This extended up a couple of dry stone-walled terraces, at the end of which had been positioned a wall of wire netting, thus preventing any escape. The unfortunate animal would be culled if young enough and sufficiently succulent for an eventual serving on the dining table.

On this latest occasion, the tension mounted. Jordi directed me to the lower level of the mountain side to help thwart any escape whilst he and my two grandchildren chased around so as to manoeuvre the hapless 3-legged goat into the trap. The plan was working brilliantly. All the adult goats, wise by now to such an act, beat a retreat along their usual escape route towards the upper more inaccessible part of the mountain. The 3-legged goat, about 6 months old, had not yet grown wise. His indecision allowed us to head him into the trap.

A perfect execution of our plan, it would seem.

Jordi, another first, scrambled up a terrace retaining wall to the head of the funnel. Jack and I were clapping for all we were worth in order to persuade the young goat to move up the funnel to its head, where by now both Jordi and Freya were awaiting its arrival.

Whilst Jordi was positioning himself in readiness for the capture, Freya, aged 9, was having other thoughts. She was thinking "This goat is not for killing, I will help it escape."

Traitor. Somehow this goat, bearing in mind it's pretty drastic disability, also had other ideas. It managed to loosen the wall of wire at the head of the trap, brushed past Freya and avoided the reaching hands of Jordi, the so-called experienced local hunter of wild goats!

A frantic chase then ensued, led by Jack, anxious to replay our strategy to capture the legless one. I've never seen a 3-legged goat move so fast. It was certainly not in any way impeded by its disability, nor was it suffering in any way as a result of its deformity. Nor, it seemed, by our antics.

Jordi by this stage was totally out of the running, due to his high level of unfitness. Freya was a happy bunny and

Jack and I were moving rapidly into position to repeat the process.

This is when the calamity happened.

At the very moment we were about to recapture the goat, the water lorry appeared along our *camino,* track. We had forgotten that Jordi had ordered another 12 tonnes of drinking water for the topping up of our fresh water tanks. Not for us in this remote spot the convenience of a mains water supply. Seeing that we were being distracted, the 3-legged goat, I swear, cocked a snoop at Jack, Jordi and myself, smiled at Freya and, without more ado, joined his parents higher up the mountain.

A very sad ending indeed.

I believe it was this incident, on reflection, which caused Jack to change sides. "Gramps" he said, "I want to capture the goat, but I don't want to eat it!"

I responded "So what do you want to do with it then?"

Back came the reply "I just want to stroke it and then let it go back to its mummy."

With this I just went into despair.

Jack is usually the first one to either hear or spot the wild goats as they emerge from the other side of the mountain moving towards our property in search of more succulent grazing.

On this particular occasion, he went charging down the stone steps leading from our terrace to the car park below shouting "There are five of them, three here and three over there."

"That's six!" corrects his sister Freya.

"Oh yes!" he agreed.

The kids had decided to categorise these regular visitors. This sighting was of the 'black family'. The 3-legged goat belonged to the 'brown family', who I suppose are distant cousins.

One hot afternoon we decided to go out stalking, yet again. We soon came across the 3-legged goat, quietly grazing as usual close to its mother. This time I was carrying my binoculars. Freya managed to stealthily move to within 20 paces and take lots of photographs.

It dawned on me, from such a close vantage point, that the poor creature had not been born with a deformity after all, or even lost its leg by accident. Rather, it had somehow dislocated its hind leg which was now seemingly firmly fixed into a position high up its rear quarter with the hoof hanging down from around the proximity of its short tail. It was quite unable to lower this leg to the ground.

One mystery solved. Jack wondered if we could catch it and take it to the vet!

Goats being clearly at the forefront of his young mind, Jack asked: "Gramps, do goats know that other goats are getting shot?"

And then: "Do people have goats as pets?"

I don't know what he had in mind, but I certainly wasn't about to encourage the conversation in this direction. It is quite easy to divert the mind of a 7 year old.

As predictable as night follows day, the hapless goat steered well away from our boundaries during all the next day. Nonetheless, Jack would venture outside our immediate confines in search of his "friend". I tried, without success, to suggest this would be fruitless.

But bravado clearly overcame the goat the following day, two days after our pathetic attempt at capture. On the way down our steps leading to the hired car I stumbled upon the said creature. It was brazenly grazing alongside our boundary fence. Its mother was in usual attendance. I found myself not 5 metres away from it but regrettably this time with no helpers to attempt a fresh capture. The children had gone out with their parents for the day.

It was clearly not in any kind of pain whatsoever in spite of its deformity. It simply accepted its lot. Of course, a wild goat having only three legs in the mountains is somewhat inconvenienced. After it was startled, it attempted a vertical retreat up a terraced wall, only to fall back down. Its mother had again scarpered, leaving its offspring to fend for itself. Had my little helpers been on hand in all probability we would have caught it. Off it trundled. It can't have too many of its nine lives left, if kids with three legs indeed have nine lives!

On another stalking mission, Jack enquired: "Gramps, are you a very good curler?"

"Whatever do you mean, Jack?"

"Can you curl up on the floor?"

"Why?" I asked hesitatingly.

"So you can get through the hole in the fence."

Jack had discovered a gap in the stone boundary wall between the two estates surrounding our property. Ever since he was a toddler he had always wished he could cross over onto the neighbouring estate to stalk the goats. After all, they always seemed to come from over there each afternoon, he had worked out.

I told him that I really couldn't curl up that well.

"Don't worry, I'll teach you to curl into a small ball." he said.

After the lesson, he decided I was quite able to ease my relatively small frame through the hole. Being unable to think of a way out of my predicament I found myself crawling on my back over sharp stones and crossing onto the neighbouring estate hoping beyond hope we would not be spotted by the owner walking his boundaries, gun in hand.

The innocence of youth.

There is yet a further twist to this tale, however.

An interesting culling opportunity occurred one day shortly after we had had the grandchildren staying with us over part of the UK school summer holidays.

I happened to hear the high pitched crying of a baby goat. They, as I have said, are the most succulent.

Well, Freya and Jack had by now become used to stalking goats with me up in the mountains behind our home. It's a thoroughly enjoyable experience. Hides are built for the grandkids to remain hidden whilst the goats come grazing nearby. That's the theory. In practice the kids make too much noise, so this game remains theoretical.

When bored, the children and I venture deep into the afforested landscape, building cairns in strategic locations to guide our way back down the complex mountain trails.

When I heard the cry, it was the morning after the children had returned back to the UK with their parents. I found a baby goat, this one being more conventional, having four legs. It was trapped in some rusty barbed wire on our boundary, bleating plaintively for its mother.

So I decided to call for Jordi. He would know how best to deal with this situation. As Jordi was helping his son in Soller he agreed to call on his way home that evening.

He arrived empty handed, that is to say, without holding any weapon in hand. When he sees the youngster still bleating he asked me whether I wanted it killed. Well, I wouldn't have hesitated, but my wife was witnessing the event so I decided I had better outline my predicament to her.

"Do we release it to the kid's mum or should I ask Jordi to see it off?"

Maggie decided to leave the decision in my hands, well knowing just how destructive wild goats can be when let loose in our garden. I decided it must not be allowed to grow older for it only to return to my garden for its daily intake of tasty food. So Jordi despatched it. Quite straight forward. No fuss.

It was removed to his place, deftly skinned, quartered and popped into his freezer. End of matter.

Except what do we tell the grandchildren about the incident?

After some deliberation, we decided that a white lie would not go amiss. The event was related to them during one of our nightly telephone conversations with them and their parents. I told Jack all the details about the baby goat and how it came to be trapped and then "rescued" by Jordi who released it to its mother.

"Gramps" he said, "why did you allow Jordi to release it? You should have asked him to kill it so that it wouldn't come back and eat your young trees!"

Kids!

Some six weeks later when my wife and I returned to the *casa* I saw the 3-legged goat grazing nonchalantly alongside our boundary. By now it had attached itself to the "black" family of goats. That morning there were eight of the blighters, some of whom had both black and brown markings. There had clearly been some inter-breeding!

My wife seemed happy at the sighting saying: "That's good news that he hasn't been killed."

To which I replied morosely "More's the pity!"

A week later, on the morning of our departure back to England, these same eight goats were found grazing around the vicinity of our car. It was as if the forest jungle drums had alerted them to the end of our short stay. Upon our leaving they simply turned their heads then returned to their breakfast. I despaired.

All these incidents clearly played on my grandson's mind. Shortly after he had started his new school at the end of that eventful summer he was chatting to my wife and suddenly said: "Gran, can we go back with you to Majorca next year, if you're still alive?"

A seven year old boy clearly thinks that being in our 60's we are positively decrepit!

Jack and Freya, Majorca 2011

Chapter 14 Footnotes

Not strictly "footnotes", more like "perspectives". What follows are insights into the workings of some organizations in the educational, voluntary and business sectors. Nothing too serious, merely a flavour, adding context to my journey.

Firstly our adoption of the island of Majorca as a place for a second home needed some work on the language, not least to avoid any backlash of xenophobia amongst the locals in the region we'd now chosen to spend most of our time.

Taking holidays in Valldemossa thus proved to be yet another watershed in my life. No English is spoken here, or very little. It was essential to learn Spanish. More so than staying in Puerto Pollensa. After gaining a GCSE when I turned 60, I decided it would be better if I could become reasonably fluent. Spending longer on the island amongst the locals was not yet a practical option.

My close working connections with Aston University in Birmingham facilitated my joining the 18-21 year old degree students for their 2 hours a week module in Spanish. Happily I was accepted by them, having been rather reticent about how I might be received.

On my first evening in class they thought, not unnaturally I suppose, that I was their tutor! Shortly into the session I soon realized that I was not easily following the tutorial. As my dear wife had previously hinted that I might be losing my hearing I decided I'd better take myself off for a test. She proved to be correct. She usually is. I was duly fitted with a hearing aid though I hasten to say this was a marginal decision. The device seemed unobtrusive, which suited me.

Now the problem I experienced was when I needed to change the battery in class. How was I to do this surreptitiously, with the class remaining oblivious to my predicament? Well unfortunately I managed to drop the tiny metal battery, which then proceeded to roll right across the floor in front of my tutor. I tried my best to appear nonchalant about the incident, though my reddening face was to give the game away.

Pleasingly, but not without much studying each week for three years, I passed my Spanish A-Level equivalent and then my finals, having taken internationally recognised Spanish examinations in the Great Hall at the University amongst some 300 other students. A pretty daunting task and another mountain climbed.

It was my work as a Chartered Surveyor dealing with the commercial sector and giving strategic advice to corporate clients regarding their property assets which led to my being asked initially to sit on the Estates Committee of Aston University.

Aston's campus lies on the edge of Birmingham city centre. To its students this is a major advantage. Such a prime location brings its own challenges, constantly causing us to weigh asset value against the academic needs of the four separate schools which form the university. To the credit of successive Vice Chancellors and the Council, the campus is "green", with a variety of attractive and sustainable new buildings contrasting with the stark brickwork of the original main building.

I was to serve on both the governing body and the Finance and Special Projects Committee, it becoming clear to me that Aston was a real gem, arguably underrated as a leading learning institution.

Add to this the fact that it is sited very close to the historic Curzon Street station where the recently announced HS2 project, the planned high speed rail link between London and Birmingham will terminate – if it ever gets completed. Either way Aston sits on a sizeable chunk of valuable real estate.

A voluntary partnership between Birmingham City Council, West Midlands Police and the private sector was founded in 1989 and known as Birmingham Citywatch. This was a UK pilot scheme for the installation of CCTV in the city centre. Its success depended on creating a membership base plus sponsorship to ensure its viability. I became chairman of the company and subsequently of the Charitable Trust which was formed to raise and handle the funding.

It started with the aid of a government grant. The idea was to install 45 state of the art colour tilt and zoom

CCTV cameras to monitor most of the principal streets in Birmingham city centre, to be operated by 4 disabled people (who were quite excellent) from monitors installed in Steelhouse Lane police station in the city centre.

The strategy was to make Birmingham city centre a safer place in which to work, shop and visit. Of course we were always being attacked by the civil liberty do-gooders. We took the strongest view that if people had nothing to hide they should not be worried. A police state this was not. At least not yet.

We were always struggling for cash to install new cameras and maintain the existing ones. The day came when we were finally scraping the bottom of the barrel, with the City Council continually saying they were unable to help. This was after we had demonstrated that there had been a real reduction in the city centre crime stats.

A dream opportunity came our way when Birmingham was asked to host the G8 Summit of the eight richest industrialized countries in the world in May 1998. The leaders of those countries would spend a few days in the city centre. These included Bill Clinton, Boris Yeltsin and Tony Blair.

Security would need to be top drawer.

The council's Chief Executive Officer at that time was Sir Michael Lyons who was later to become chairman of the BBC Trust. I well recall my conversation with him at a hurriedly called meeting in his office behind closed doors.

I said: "We need £40,000 to keep the cameras rolling, otherwise we have to close them down immediately."

Mike Lyons responded: "How soon do you want it Glyn?"

Job done.

Machiavellian? Maybe, but effective. This funding would last us two years.

One of my most satisfying periods working within the voluntary sector was when I joined the fund-raising committee of St. Basils, a well-known Birmingham based charity working with young people aged between 16 and 25 to prevent youth homelessness by providing accommodation and support services. Nowadays not too many people are sleeping rough on the streets of Birmingham, thanks largely to the really excellent work done by this organization.

Within that age profile are young mums and dads. This consequently necessitates the housing also of babies and children.

Homelessness has many causes including abuse, overcrowding and family breakdown. The charity works across Birmingham, Solihull and North Worcestershire and both supports and encourages young people to enter further education or find a job. This enables them ultimately to learn how to live independently and support themselves financially.

I always wondered why many of the homeless are seen on street corners with pet dogs quietly lying obediently at their side. It was only after helping St Basils and becoming interested in their plight that it became apparent: their dogs are often their best friends, being loyal and trustworthy, sadly unlike their owners' experiences with the human race.

I learned that 1 in 20 young people in Birmingham fall into homelessness every year.

I know this is a problem throughout the UK. So I do like to support the street vendors we have become accustomed to seeing around our city centres selling the weekly "Big Issue". I see this as not giving a hand-out but rather a hand-up. It is a way of giving homeless people the opportunity of making their own money. The bonus is that this magazine is not just helping the vendor but actually is well produced, often containing some really interesting articles on wide-ranging subjects.

During my involvement with St. Basils I agreed to engage in two particular fundraising activities which appealed to my sense of adventure: sleeping rough on the street and being locked up in jail.

I somehow managed to persuade my son Simon to join me on the sleep-out along with the Business Editor of the

Birmingham Post, John Duckers – well, we needed publicity to raise money. And cometh the hour, cometh the man! This is an annual event organized by St. Basils. The charity or one of their sponsors provides the cardboard. The trick is to arrive before nightfall at the appointed location, an empty car park near the centre of Birmingham, select an acceptable pitch and build a cardboard shelter which becomes the roof over your head for one night. This event takes place deliberately at the end of November. It's pure masochism!

Our particular night was pitch black, extremely cold and drizzly. Having built our respective shelters the three of us quietly retreated off-site in search of a curry which would set us up for the long night ahead. We returned about midnight when most of the participants had already settled down. Regrettably Simon in the dark tripped over his neighbour's makeshift shelter which turned out to be occupied by the then Bishop of Aston. Apologies were duly proffered and readily accepted.

Eventually we settled down, sleeping only fitfully, the drizzle having turned into incessant rain which found pathways leading inside my cardboard roof now sagging about 3 inches above my nose. And John's snoring alongside my pitch was troublesome. But it was all worth it. We managed to raise over £1500 for the charity.

The other fundraising event was a tough challenge.

Steelhouse Police Station is a Victorian building in the centre of Birmingham. It's not terribly comfortable. That's putting it mildly! I've spent much time there working in another capacity with a number of former Chief Constables, but never locked up! The idea was to make a number of phone calls from inside the basement jail to friends and business colleagues so as to obtain pledges securing £1000 for my release.

Needless to say a great many of my so called "friends" offered to donate more money to persuade the police to keep me incarcerated!

Much of my activity with Aston University was undertaken on a voluntary basis. This seems to come with the territory of working in the professional sector. The private sector is encouraged to put something back into the society from whence it derives a living.

In this vein and following a vote within the business community I was elected to represent our region as its business representative on the Birmingham, Coventry and Black Country City Region board.

I was to report back to the then named West Midlands Business Council soon to become Business Voice West Midlands. After serving a three year term I stood down at the country's 2010 General Election shortly before the City Region was disbanded in favour of the setting up of the latest political flavour of the month, a Local Enterprise Partnership.

Following the demise of the Regional Development Agencies, funding to such business umbrella groups as

BVWM was to be withdrawn, thus throwing its future into uncertainty.

Being on the City Region board was to prove a real eye-opener. I was to work closely with the Leaders of the seven Metropolitan District Councils including the Leader of Birmingham City Council who chaired the board and their respective Chief Executive Officers. This was indeed a poisoned chalice.

To encourage these disparate authorities to work together as a team supporting Birmingham as the obvious engine room for the region was to liken this with treading on eggshells. Sycophancy is not one of my conscious traits. Never being one to tread lightly a few eggshells were crushed when I suggested that the City Region's cumbersome name be simplified to the Greater Birmingham City Region to help better identify the region internationally.

Unsurprisingly the other local authorities would have none of it.

The concept of a true partnership, working together in harmony, for the greater economic benefit of the region was shot to ribbons at the very outset. I had overlooked the fact that I was dealing with politicians who paid scant regard for the region's longer term good in favour of jockeying for their own short-term position within the hierarchy of this public sector.

After enduring three years of hearing why we could not implement economic policies to create jobs and encourage private enterprise I had had enough. These politicians together with their officers favoured the setting up of endless consultative committees and working parties rather than taking positive decisions and implementing the necessary actions. This became a constant battle of process over progress. The former invariably won, I'm afraid.

I decided my time would be better spent doing other things as opposed to witnessing these so-called leaders and chief executives paying mere lip service to perfectly plausible strategies coming from the private sector.

One such strategy I tried to champion was the urgent rolling out of superfast broadband across our region.

I argued within the highly charged City Region forum how this could be done within a tight timeframe and limited budget. The region would steal a march from other regions all of whom were in competition with ourselves to attract new inward investment, both nationally and internationally. I had a plan, having widely consulted with possible stakeholders. I presented to the City Region board and my proposals were accepted. But unfortunately the bureaucratic process then cut in to thwart implementation.

In spite of strenuous efforts I made to present viable action plans supporting economic regeneration and job creation, progress stalled. The 2010 General Election was then called and everything shut down!

How naïve of me to believe that the economic rejuvenation of a region could continue seamlessly whilst we entered a politically changing climate.

During this time I was becoming increasingly involved in the Birmingham Civic Society. This was like a breath of fresh air. Here, a number of volunteers from the business community along with many individual members of the Society strive to influence and improve civic pride in the city of Birmingham.

There is an interesting Maori proverb: *"If I am comfortable with where I am in the present and confident with where I shall be in the future, it is only because I am standing on the shoulders of the past."*

This to me sounded plausible. I could see how a body of trustees, sitting on the Council of the Birmingham Civic Society, could add value to the city by actively promoting high standards of planning and architecture, the city's heritage, the active management of a tree planting programme and the stimulation of the minds of hundreds of young people in local schools through the Society's citizenship programme.

As a vice-chairman I was to sit on a small working group which was helping to deliver new strategies to a society founded in 1918. Well established business contacts were encouraged to join their companies into our organisation. With enormous help and guidance from the Royal College of Arms in London we designed, found sponsors and were awarded in 2008, our 90th year, a Grant of Arms, using as our motto "*Pro civitate*", meaning "For the citizens". We were also grateful to the city council for its support.

This was to be a first for Birmingham among the country's many civic societies.

Arms and crests are granted by letters patent. The Crown delegates its authority to issue such letters patent

to the Kings of Arms who are officers of the College of Arms. It's all terribly English, steeped in history. And a great honour to be conferred a Grant of Arms. Moreover, and this is an essential pre-requisite, we were well supported in Birmingham by the Honorary City Armorist.

The culmination of this work was a prestigious ceremony held in Birmingham's Victorian Council House when the Letters Patent were presented to us formally by the Lancaster Herald, presided over by our President, the Lord Mayor of Birmingham.

It's worth recording here, as it will not generally be known, that the Birmingham Civic Society became involved in submitting designs for street furniture and telephone boxes back in 1937. Our designs which were used in a national competition led to the production of the iconic red telephone boxes which Britain is well known for.

I was deputed with another vice-chairman Anthony Collins to grow our corporate membership. We decided that we needed a hundred firms as a minimum to give us a worthwhile critical mass. One pragmatic idea to aid this ambition was to secure a sponsor or two and organise a couple of corporate networking events from where we would attract companies into joining the Civic Society.

So far as I am aware, Birmingham is the only UK city which has a corporate membership list in addition to its individual members. Presently this has grown to over

100 firms and we have notable sponsors for our two corporate events which are now happily ensconced in our annual diary of events.

One such event is badged as the Leader's Breakfast.

Over the last 5 years we have packed a room at the Hotel du Vin in the city centre and each year the Leader of the City Council would update us on progress over the last year and announce aspirations over the coming year. What a prestigious event this has become.

On this last occasion I was asked to open the early morning meeting by introducing a special guest who was to address the packed room before breakfast was served and prior to the Leader's presentation. Griff Rhys Jones happens to be the current President of Civic Voice, the national charity for the civic movement in England. Their objective is to promote civic pride. How worthwhile is that?

Griff is remembered as one half of that classic TV comedy series, "Alas Smith and Jones" in the 1980's and 1990's.

Quite apart from being a Welsh comedian, he is an actor, a writer, a TV presenter and a champion of architecture, both ancient and modern. Being a graduate of Cambridge and a raconteur extraordinaire, his riposte to my indicating we wouldn't mention the Rugby World Cup was that he might be considered as being only a mere Welshman from Epping....Well Griff sat me down just 5 minutes before I was due to introduce him and asked why he was here and what he should say to the great and the good of Birmingham.

I tried my best not to panic. I hurriedly briefed him. As always we were on an extremely tight timescale. Following my introduction he rose and, in the inimitable, effusive style of this presently bearded wonder, he opened with:

"Thank you Glyn for your kind words of introduction. I can't wait to hear what I've got to say!"

Howls of laughter from the attentive audience. Little did they know!

I was flanked between him and the Lord Bishop of Birmingham. During breakfast the three of us lamented about the absence of members in the audience from the ethnic communities, Griff having observed that all faces in the room were white. My companions did however agree that arguably this issue is the biggest challenge we face as a Civic Society.

Somehow we have to create a culture bridge encouraging a more multi-cultural mix of invitees. However hard we've tried, it has proved pretty difficult to persuade business people of other ethnic groups to join us in any meaningful quantity. We will persevere and hope one day to succeed.

To its credit, business is continually encouraging both its leaders and staff to engage with us in promoting worthwhile community projects.

Happily we also work closely with, though not funded by, and rightly so, the City Council. Involvement from individuals contributes to their personal development, which clearly helps employers when considering progression in companies. We try to generate new corporate membership by using appointed ambassadors and by organising networking events engaging the services of high profile speakers happy to support the Society, almost always without cost.

For those interested in personal development, opportunities to become involved in a wide variety of such activities are many. And the outcomes are truly satisfying.

Griff Rhys Jones, the author and
the Lord Bishop of Birmingham

Chapter 15 More Nuptials

"*Este verano nos casamos.*" "This summer we are getting married," it said on the invitation we received from our young friends Jose Luis and Sandra.

We were introduced to Jose Luis some three years ago. He is a Majorcan builder, the son of Pepin who founded this well established and reputable building company and who has now handed over to his son. Pepin is about 60 and, like his son, speaks only Castilian Spanish and Majorcan. No English, or very little.

Having retired from his company, Pepin has reinvented himself as a most accomplished contemporary painter. Working from a studio at his modern home he had built himself in Marratxi near Santa Maria, he has now begun showing his paintings in Palma galleries.

His work is so remarkable that only this last year he won both first and second places for paintings he had done for the design of posters advertising the Fiesta of St Juan 2011 in Menorca – an annual festival held each June of Menorcan horsemen riding through the streets of this smaller Balearic island, including the riding of horses through the homes of residents. Imagine doing that in England!

This spectacle seems particularly popular with Majorcans who take the short ferry ride from Alcudia to Cuidadella, the former capital of Menorca, in order to witness these antics culminating in all night parties on the beaches. Pepin's original oil painting, depicting a horse's head in sombre blue and black tones with flashes of red, now hangs in the hall of the island's former capital's *ajuntamiento*, the Town Hall.

Pepin arrived at our *finca* accompanied by both his son and fiancée Sandra who speaks impeccable English. They had come to help me with a project involving the possible diversion of a *camino*, or track, leading from the Valldemossa – Deià road to the steps which lead up to the house. A short detour of this track along the terraced landscape would substantially reduce the number of steps to be climbed in order to arrive at ours.

As the region has recently obtained World Heritage Site status, it would be necessary to seek appropriate local authority and government permission before attempting such works.

They had also come to present us with a wedding invitation and to thoughtfully hand over a copy of Pepin's poster which was specially selected to promote the 2011 Menorcan Fiesta.

The 13th August 2011 finally arrived; the eagerly awaited wedding day. The island was in the middle of a heatwave, daytime temperatures reaching 37 degrees centigrade. The civil ceremony conducted in Castilian Spanish was being held in the grounds of a 14th century former monastery in the country, close to the town of Binissalem. The immaculately tendered grounds had water features which could have been designed by the Moors from North Africa who at that time occupied the island.

Unlike at home in England, everything was arranged to take place outside, in the evening when the air temperature had cooled to a comfortable 27 degrees. The bride arrived in a vintage Rolls Royce. Maggie and I were the only English guests. Quite an honour, we thought. The remaining 170 guests were largely Majorcan, though many came from mainland Spain and Germany, being family and friends of the beautiful bride who was born to a distinguished Majorcan father and an attractive German mother.

The couple were led along a purple carpet by two infants, a nephew and niece, to a florally decorated wedding gazebo positioned alongside a mature pine. They clearly enjoyed throwing handfuls of rose petals ahead of the bride and groom. Following the ceremony, the children were called upon to hand over the rings and then, to the surprise of all, a box was handed over which was opened to release a number of colourful butterflies to the obvious pleasure of the entire gathering.

At the end of the ceremony we were all invited to congratulate the bride and groom. All lady guests were each given an *abanico*, a fan, adorned with the names of Sandra and Jose Luis, which in view of the heat was to prove useful as the celebrations continued, though I had noticed that many of the Spanish ladies had brought along their own.

A beautifully adorned courtyard romantically lit by candles was laid out for dinner which was served at around 10.30pm. Appetisers consisting of a variety of tapas much loved by the Spanish preceded the wedding banquet of a fish starter, followed by *solomillo argentino de ternera,* a fillet of Argentinean steak and a *tarta de chocolate blanco,* white chocolate cake, washed down with wines from local bodegas and an Anna de Codorniu *cava reserva.*

Entertainment started with a Majorcan friend, Vicente, who works with Jose Luis, playing his Spanish guitar, to be joined by an American singer in the style of Madeleine Peyroux. A different trio played through dinner, followed by a DJ with dancing through until about 5am.

My rendering of "Guantanamera," the Cuban folk song, in Spanish, with Pepin, the groom's affable father, as a duet, backed by the builder-cum-Spanish guitar player Vicente, could perhaps have been more polished. But by then however, it was about 3am and we were a bit worse for wear.

Maybe we should have eased back a bit on the *Suau,* that excellent brandy from nearby Marratxi.

The Flamenco dancing by another of Jose Luis' friends, joined by other guests, was brilliant.

During *cena*, or dinner, the banter with our German friends was entertaining and I was persuaded to sing Lili

Marlene, in English, whilst a wonderfully talented and buxom German fraulein joined me in a duet.

I tried not to mention two subjects, the war and football, preferring to steer the subject to cricket. England were trouncing the Indians to overtake them as being the best cricket team in the World. Our German friends tried to say that we were the *only* team in the World! What do they know!

Anyway, they can talk. I read in the local newspaper about a strangely serious body in Germany called the Etiquette Society. This body is apparently calling for a workplace kissing ban! Only the Europeans could dream up this one. Instead it advises that colleagues should shake hands from a distance of around 60 cm. They believe that most females don't like kissing. They somehow feel there is an erotic aspect to it, a form of body contact which can be used by men to get close to a woman. The Society suggests that those workers who do not want a peck on the cheek should place a sign on their desks indicating a 'no kissing' zone, preferring a traditional handshake. Whatever next?

The following day was blisteringly hot, the heatwave set to continue. Wall to wall sunshine punctuated only by high cumulus cloud. My hangover wasn't too bad, surprising really. I did however decide to stay out of the sun, preferring to write this account under the dapple shade of an ancient olive tree on our upper terrace, the happy couple having joined a Mediterranean cruise from Palma for their honeymoon.

Majorcans don't like to travel too far from home. Wherever they go I feel they prefer to keep their island in sight.

Could this have possibly been inherited from their antecedents who were, after all, invaded on several occasions, usually when they were sleeping, thus engendering a desire to protect their beautiful homeland?

I couldn't blame them for that.

Chapter 16 Tramuntana

The *Serra de Tramuntana* in Majorca which is the largest island in the archipelago known as the Balearic Islands, runs on an axis from the south-west to the north-east of the island. This stretches about 90km, the mountain range representing a zone of great ecological value.

Inappropriate commercial development for the tourist industry, particularly in the south, gained the island a certain notoriety. A tour along the northerly mountain road gives a more complete perspective and helps redress this sorry reputation.

Tramuntana also happens to be the classical name for a cold, dry, northern wind.

Deservedly so, this region has just been awarded World Heritage Status by UNESCO.

The name "Balearics" traces its origin to the early inhabitants of the island who had a peculiar fighting mode which involved a sling. Thus in about 300BC the Greeks and the Phoenicians were inspired to name the archipelago "Balearides" I understand because the word "ballein" in Greek means "to throw a sling".

The Coastline along the *Serra de Tramuntana* is very rugged with a few sandy but mainly rocky coves and sheer limestone cliffs falling vertically into the sea. It can be treacherous, inhospitable terrain and understandably is the region with most water on this island. Driving along some of the narrow roads is not for the faint-hearted.

Along the way are *fuentes*, fountains, built into the stone retaining wall where locals stop to fill their containers with precious drinking water percolating from the summits. An ancient custom and right.

One of the best ways to appreciate its scale is by boat but the area is also extremely popular with walkers and cyclists. Snow can fall on these mountains annually, the highest peak being Puig Major (1,477m) which is just higher than Ben Nevis, the highest mountain in the British Isles.

When the Moors of North Africa invaded Spain in the eighth century there followed a chapter of horror and suppression which lasted over centuries. This notwithstanding, some good came out of this unwanted occupation which is plain for all to see today, particularly in this region.

Mainly in the southern half of Spain the Moors went on to construct some of Europe's finest cities such as Seville, Cordoba, Toledo and Granada. The Alhambra in Granada is a sight to behold, tempered somewhat by the sheer volume of tourists throughout the year shuffling their way through the ancient palaces and the well-planned gardens with their elaborate gravity-fed irrigation channels and numerous water features taking full advantage of the natural contours.

Thus when the Moors conquered the Balearic Islands they began to introduce their own culture and develop the economy. This was to be achieved largely in peace alongside the Jews and Christians. This influence can be witnessed all around Majorca though is especially prevalent in the north.

Terraces were dug in the steeply sloping fields facing the northern coastline, with retaining walls built of local stone which was in abundant supply. Olive groves and a variety of fruit trees were planted and expertly irrigated, making use of falling rainwater and melting snow. I am hugely impressed with Deià's system of open natural irrigation channels. And the typical gardens, particularly of the *haciendas*, estate houses and the boutique country hotels remain essentially architectural, combining the Islamic influence of water and the use of stone and statuary, interjected with 1000 year old gnarled olive trees and deep green twisted carobs.

West of Valldemossa the small coastal town of Banyalbufar also bears witness to this, meaning "Vineyard by the Sea" or, in Arabic, *bany al buhar*. Here, up until the end of the nineteenth century when they were wiped out by disease, vines were cultivated on the terraced slopes which step down to the sea. Now vegetables have taken their place, making full use of the irrigation system.

It was not until the re-birth of wine growing began as late as the 1990's that Majorcan wines were put on the map. Before then the wine lacked finesse and much was imported from the Spanish mainland. The island wine is now largely produced in three areas: Binissalem, this being the best known, found on the plains coming off the Tramuntana mountains, Pla and Llevant, on the central plains where the Romans originally planted the vines and Serra de Tramuntana and Costa Nord.

The mountains create a microclimate for vineyards in this region, thus making the resulting wines distinctive to the area. I find them not particularly cheap but the quality has enormously improved and definitely worth buying. In my view this is also true of Spanish wines from the mainland, a huge improvement over the last two decades.

The region is also privileged in enjoying a richness of flora and fauna which attracts specialist interest from botanists and birdwatchers alike.

In the mountains behind our *casa* are very many former charcoal kilns, raised flat earth beds encased in dry stone walling. Here the local charcoal burners over a century ago would camp out in these mountains in rough stone shelters adjoining their kilns to burn the pine and holm oak to make the charcoal. They would haul this by mule and cart down into the towns, villages and hamlets to sell to the local inhabitants to heat up their homes.

As electricity was introduced onto the island in the early twentieth century such activity naturally dwindled.

Once the railway line reached Soller only a hundred years ago, the island's Government began planning its roads across the Tramuntana mountain range. This was to challenge the engineers. It was an Italian engineer who went on to design and build a road taking account of the natural contours, introducing hairpin bends rather than merely dynamiting his way through the mountains.

My active mind wandered back to the days when pirates made constant raids on this side of the island between the 14th and 17th centuries. These would be Moors, often assaulting their victims in the middle of the night. Their hostages would be taken and sold as slaves in the North African markets. Even today the Port of Valldemossa still attracts smugglers due to its remoteness and particularly difficult access.

Thankfully I am not aware of any present-day marauders and bandits landing and creating havoc by employing their favourite pastime of raping and pillaging.

Such raids are vividly re-enacted each year by the local citizens, dressed in appropriate costumes of the era, in the ports of Soller and Pollensa, watched in awe by hundreds of tourists. Back then the inhabitants decided to make themselves more secure by moving their homes a few miles inland. Thus the towns of Soller and Pollensa were developed, with watchtowers being built along this rugged coastline to ward off the marauders.

These days the area is famous for its tourist train from Palma to Soller and on to its port. The partly open-sided train passes leisurely through the mountains past fields of almond trees and olive groves to Soller station which opened in 1912. Originally powered by steam, the engines were electrified back in 1929, the line being built to carry the town's principal export, oranges.

Living here, as we do when we are on the island, life seems to slow down. The tranquillity seems somehow deafening, punctuated by wonderful birdsong. The noise from the main mountain road some 100m below us is a mere accompaniment to thought.

So with few distractions opportunities abound to delve into one's inner self. Some would call this daydreaming. The mind can wander into dangerous territory as the following mischievous thoughts highlight:

As I move inexorably into the murky twilight zone of *really* old age, I began wondering if I may be more suited to joining the club of grumpy old men. At least, that's what I keep being told by my wife and grandkids. Isn't this a bit unfair however? Below the belt, even.

It is certainly true that I do tend to hate magpies and foxes back in the UK and particularly wild mountain goats here. But don't most people? Are we really happy standing in a queue at any bar or supermarket waiting to be served? Or as a motorist arriving at a pelican crossing where the lights have just turned to red with no-one in sight or after someone has already crossed and is seen disappearing into the sunset!

The prince in "Cinderella" being played by a female has to me even as a child always seemed incongruous. At the risk of sounding misogynistic, why wouldn't it be a man?

Some benefits must be derived from spending a reasonable amount of time in the relative solitude of the Tramuntana mountains.

In my case, in a pique of soliloquy whilst enjoying a few days on the island prior to Maggie joining me, I decided to fantasize a "Man of the Month" award.

That's probably illegal these days. Political correctness dictates this should be called "Person of the Month", but I prefer the use of the noun "man" generically, in the context of describing a human. This is why I prefer the term "chairman" rather than "chair", which surely is an object. "Chairperson" is too cumbersome. And whoever thinks of "landlady and tenant" in the context of "landlord and tenant"?

My rules would open such an award to any man or woman of any nationality, religion, job or profession. Even to politicians, economists and estate agents, whether from Birmingham or Bangkok. The award would not be material, in the form of a silver cup or monetary payment. It would simply be honorary, prestigious and good for the curriculum vitae though arguably not much else!

It would acknowledge absolute prowess or achievement on the one hand or alternatively abject apathy even stupidity on the other.

The right would be reserved not to make such an award each month, but only given to deserving applicants as and when they arise. Nominations would be open for consideration by a panel of three eminent judges. That is, if three could be found!

I would publish a list both of nominees and recipients of the award, doubtless on Facebook, holidays, illness or total apathy permitting.

Past winners might have been: Tony Blair for cocking up the whole of the Middle East; Sir Michael Lyons for successfully handing over the BBC Trust baton to another applicant, Lord Patten, who equally knows sod all about the running of a television company, and the ITV Executive for suspending the writer of the popular TV series "Midsomer Murders" for excluding any coloured person from the series' distinct rural English setting.

I'm with Pericles when he proffered: "Wait for that wisest of counsellors, Time."

It must be the Majorcan sun which seems to titillate my imagination.

Naturally the climate is noticeably cooler than on the plains, which in the summer heat is a blessing. It is said that every 200m rise above sea level gives a drop of 1 degree centigrade.

The locals are friendly yet reserved, where the guttural sounding dialect of the language derived from the Catalan region of north-eastern Spain resonates in all the towns and villages along this stretch of the island.

The sheer delight experienced when a cinnamon coloured hoopoe is spotted darting from tree to tree or a pair of eagles are seen at high altitude gliding effortlessly on the strong current of the Tramuntana winds.

So, by now, you probably have a reasonable picture of this region, a paradigm of alpine landscapes yet having a distinctive character of its own and why the police are ever vigilant regarding the spotting of possible unauthorised fires.

Even during October, supposedly the autumn, forest fires can still wreak havoc if, as often happens, the dry summer period extends beyond its acknowledged time, failing to defer to a cooler season.

If never visited, then this region should be entered on your list of unforgettable places to see before you die!

Chapter 17 Sa Foradada

Majorca as an island, its indigenous population and its delightfully different varieties of cuisine, never cease to amaze me. The local English newspaper, published six days a week, is the Majorcan Daily Bulletin. It has quite a big following. It is considered by most expatriates as the equivalent of the quintessentially English tabloid. Essential reading over breakfast. For some. Certainly I put my wife into this category of loyal readers.

Unlike my wife who would go out of her way to spend a euro on this newspaper, I have discovered that the local tourist office hands out the MDB free of charge to unsuspecting punters. I tend to arrive early when the office has not yet opened for the day. The tourist coaches do not generally reach Valldemossa before 9.30 am each morning.

So I have struck up an arrangement with an extremely pleasant lady who hails from Seville but now lives in the *pueblo*. She arrives at the tourist office quite early to tidy up before it opens. Her Spanish is so clear that I enjoy practising on improving my fluency by chatting with her whilst Jordi goes off to buy his bread and order our coffee in the local bar. As she sees me striding towards the office she hands me a copy of the MDB. Job done!

Back at our *casa* I mistakenly deigned to offer my opinion on the weather.

"The strong winds are sure to bring the clouds over the island tomorrow," I exclaimed.

"No," responded Maggie, "according to the MDB the forecast over the next few days is for sun and clear skies."

I wisely deferred to my wife's more superior knowledge than mine, realising I was putting myself up against the MDB, though I quietly noted that clouds did actually appear late the following day.

Just occasionally this unique newspaper comes up with an absolute pearl of wisdom. From our bedroom window we look out onto a rock with a hole, jutting out into the sea. It is known as Sa Foradada. The hole uniquely takes the shape of the island.

This promontory is famous, particularly amongst Spanish tourists from the mainland, but also to those fortunate enough to own their own boats of all shapes and sizes. It can be reached by foot with prior permission, readily given, by descending down from the side of Son Marroig, now a museum and formerly the home of a famous Austrian naval explorer called Archduke Lluis Salvador.

The Archduke, a descendant of the Austrian Royal Family, discovered this side of the island in the late 19th century. He liked it so much that he bought estates, built

Son Marroig as a country house and settled here, also building from local stone a number of viewpoints of both the sea and the mountains. Facing due west Son Marroig looks out over spectacular sunsets. These days the tourist coaches and visitors by car come in droves, attracted by both the museum's rich heritage and the magnificent panoramic views.

From this vantage point we can just make out the distinctive home of Michael Douglas and Catherine Zeta-Jones, also built by the Archduke, just a kilometre from where we live. They are usually in residence for part of the summer.

So, I return to my tale about the MDB, as the English newspaper is so affectionately known.

My wife spotted an article about Sa Foradada and the fact that at the foot of this rock nestled in a natural harbour created by the promontory is an open air bar-cum-restaurant serving a refreshing drink called *sangria* with local freshly caught seafood, or their speciality *paella* prepared and cooked in enormous flat pans.

Access is somewhat more challenging than the usual method of simply driving to your chosen restaurant. If not arriving by boat, the trek down from the side of Son Marroig museum takes about 45 minutes or more by foot. It is quite steep and the route is unsurfaced and rugged. In fact, it's not for the faint-hearted, as the journey back up to the Valldemossa-Deià road takes at least an hour. But thanks to the MDB its well kept secret is out.

This paper failed however to mention the real possibility of jelly fish lurking in the clear blue water, awaiting unsuspecting bathers. So, kids beware!

My son Chris and his wife Alison, having read the newspaper article set aside by my wife, decided to take the trek down, quite fancying a lunch of *paella* cooked on an open wood fire. *Paella* is one of my favourite dishes. It is said to have originated from Valencia, in about the mid-nineteenth century, made from rice and seafood or meat, usually rabbit, chicken or pork, or often mixed, with green vegetables added along with a generous amount of saffron which turns the rice a golden yellow.

Home-made red wine or better still *sangria* can be served to wash it down, this being a potent mix of red wine, spirits and fruit.

Alternatively the Spanish lady proprietor from nearby Port Soller, who makes the tricky daily journey down to the rock in her 4x4 vehicle during the summer months with her helpers, will cook to order any other fish or seafood caught that day in the Soller bay. She has also laid out an open air bar for her thirsty clients who, having placed their food order, have the choice of swimming off the rocks or sunbathing whilst their meal is being freshly cooked. The *gambas al ajillo*, giant prawns caught locally, cooked in olive oil and garlic, are to die for!

Paradise, except perhaps for those having to make their way back up to their car almost 1000 feet above sea level. No such problems for those, and there are many, arriving by boat. Recently two sailing boats approached the secluded cove. It was a wedding party, dressed in period costume. The couple were to be "unofficially" married at the restaurant, prior to sitting down to a *paella* luncheon before sailing back to the Port of Soller for the official wedding.

One morning, I happened to mention our adventure to Jordi. He'd never thought of telling us it existed! He nonchalantly told me that he knew the family who founded the restaurant. Moreover he floored me when he told me that his wife Polita had worked down there, many years ago. It's no wonder she has an excellent reputation for cooking marvellously tasty *paellas*.

I believe Jordi when he said it was the daily walk down, but particularly the trek back up the hill which did it in for Polita. And you'd have to believe this, were you ever to meet her!

I should just also mention the plan I hatched to coax my little grandson back up the steep climb to where our car was parked.

Until recently he attended St. Alphege Church of England Infant School in Solihull close to where we now live. The school's music teacher is very hot on teaching the kids new songs, particularly about Jesus or about life's journey. So I asked Jack what songs he knew. He decided on the way up to sing his entire repertoire. When it comes to singing in tune he's as bad as his gramps. We are both tone deaf unlike his sister Freya who has an absolutely angelic voice which is a delight to listen to.

So Jack, for the best part of the hour it took to get us back up to the road, decided to teach me his songs. I had a spring in my stride, just, I admit, to get me home quicker! Only kidding! It was actually great fun.

At the beginning of this book I show the lyrics to one of the songs Jack taught me to sing on this trek up, called "Every Journey." The tune is haunting, the lyrics marvellous. Simple and apposite.

I don't mind admitting to all he is my *very* best friend.

Sa Foradada

Chapter 18 Dessert

In the 1970's we used to take our summer holidays camping with our two boys either in Cornwall or on the Costa Brava. In those days Spain had not yet gained its excellent reputation for outstanding Mediterranean food and for that matter, wine, particularly the reds which were rather rough. Cheap, but rough.

The country was visited by English families largely because it was cheap and cheerful, with guaranteed sunshine.

When we discovered Majorca in the late 1980's Puerto Pollensa was an unspoilt, underdeveloped town on the north-east coast. We found the odd *panaderia*, bakery, for our freshly-baked daily bread. The local wines however had not reached a good enough quality and those from the *peninsular*, the mainland, were not yet up to the quality of the French wines.

This situation has now changed greatly. The Spanish have really worked on this. The country was beginning to clean up its act, post Franco. Even the local wines from three different wine growing regions on the island were improving vastly, year on year. Today they really are excellent. Whilst the Spanish mainland has a number of distinctive wine-growing regions I particularly enjoy the reds from *Rioja, Navarra and Ribera del Duero*.

And this island is a now a gold mine when it comes to local cuisine. Even the hotel industry has made an effort, many buildings built centuries ago such as monasteries, olive mills and farm houses having been converted into small but high quality boutique hotels thanks to government grants. Their imaginative conversion, with careful preservation of original features make them a real delight to visit, if only for morning coffee or afternoon tea and home-made cake. Many such businesses now exist in the Tramuntana Mountains.

Such culinary delights we have experienced around the island generally seem to have whetted my appetite for trying my hand at cooking back home in England. I know, a little late to start perhaps, but surely better late than never, don't you think?

It was Christmas day 2010 when I opened a present from my wife Maggie.

A note inside said *"this gift voucher allows you to enjoy the services of the Pudding Pie Cookery School, based in Oxfordshire."*

My wife had clearly decided enough's enough. After 43 years of marriage I should stop *talking* about cooking and start putting it into practice. She had enrolled me onto a basic cookery course. I managed to avoid taking any action until I was reminded that my enrolment would lapse if I did not sign up within 6 months.

Quite naturally there was no way my wife would let me off the hook. This might bear some relation to the tone of my wedding anniversary cards I received last summer.

Broadly, they went something along the lines of: cue wife stringing husband upside down on a heavily weighted torture scaffold: The caption from wife's mouth read *"I'm not upset with you, just very disappointed."*

And two women chatting to each other: *"My family's all grown up now, except my husband of course."*

Try this one which I found written on a birthday card which my wife was sending to a friend. It depicted an elderly Victorian lady reclining on her chaise long, saying to her husband upon entering their sitting room:

Wife: *"My aerobics teacher says I've got the breasts of a 20 year old."*
　　　Husband: *"Did he mention your flabby arse?"*
　　　Wife: *"No dear, we never talked about you!"*

It's really unfair and below the belt.

Taking the hint, I found myself, reluctantly driving down the M40 Motorway from Solihull to attend the course. I'd set off with much trepidation, cursing myself for buying all those glossy cookbooks at bargain basement prices and following Masterchef and Jamie Oliver on television.

I do admit to having a particular weakness. This is well known to all our friends we visit but particularly Mike and Bojana, Ron and Barbara and Nick and Deena whose three young grandchildren Izzy, Heidi and Lily Mae endearingly call me "Colonel Custard."

Home made custard. That's my weakness. It is kind of an unwritten rule or should I say custom that following the main course when out at friends for lunch or dinner there is usually a jug of custard served up to me with a suitable pudding to accompany it. My all time favourite is steamed treacle sponge pudding with a bowl full of custard. Lots of treacle with lots of custard. I freely admit that all other desserts pale into insignificance.

So occasionally custard tends to be the emphasis in the odd cook book I might receive for birthday or Christmas.

The mistake my well-meaning friendliest of friends make is that they pre-suppose I might actually progress to making my own custard at home. Big mistake! I prefer to leave the custard-making to others. I ask for little, just that they lovingly mix the custard ingredients as my mother used to do. Merely buying tins of powder from the nearest supermarket simply will not do. It's not really good enough.

The devil is in the detail. Quality of the eggs is all important. Each egg must first be tested for freshness by suspending it in a pan of water. A fresh egg will sink whereas an older or stale egg will float.

I'm sure our friends engage these techniques though I suspect my wife doesn't. Can't think why not!

Also, and this is important, I rather like my custard made of the correct consistency, not too thick but not too thin, with reasonable, not overdone, sweetness. Essentially it should be lump-free. The mix has to be heated gently and stirred sufficiently, never neglecting it, however tempted, to attend to other culinary duties.

The making of pure golden custard is a real art. I personally suspect a dying one, sadly. An expert recognises when custard has not been lovingly made. It is obvious. The egg whites and the yolks will not coagulate evenly. Free-range eggs are essential. Anything less seriously impairs quality and for all I know may seriously damage one's health, particularly mine!

Maybe inferior custard should come with a health warning, only to be consumed in desperation! I like to think that my eggs which go into the mix devolve from hens lovingly cared for and which enjoy the freedom which comes from the ability to scratch around outside during daylight hours.

When we are dining out at friends' homes I truly appreciate the enormous dedication and effort put in to the making of this golden nectar. My real challenge at the table is to deter the others from partaking, thus ensuring a generous helping is at hand, particularly when anticipating seconds...

The problem I seem to be getting is that other guests are now beginning to feel they are missing something and so are electing to have custard, which really puts me out. This makes me grumpy.

I have even discovered first hand that Nick and Deena's grandkids are developing a likeness for the golden liquid.

Especially Heidi! Even Jack decided he would have some during a recent fireworks party at his home. I'm not fooled by the angelic veneer of these young creatures. I can see trouble boiling in the pan!

From this account you can now understand exactly why I was bestowed with the endearing title of Colonel Custard by the kids. Well, I think it's an endearment. Isn't it?

I was keeping to the speed limit; there seemed no point in arriving at the school too early. Anyway, wasn't I too old to join a cookery course?

Somehow, I managed not to get lost in the depths of Oxfordshire, my heart sinking when I finally arrived at the appointed hour to read the school's strapline on the notice board which indicated "*Classes to suit all ages.*" There was no obvious escape.

I was immediately offered a Nespresso americano and homemade biscuits, no doubt to calm my nerves.

I'd taken along the heavily illustrated Marie Claire Seasonal Kitchen cookbook which I'd bought at less than half price a year earlier – excellent value, except it is Canadian, which I hadn't realised at the time of purchase and with strange sounding ingredients when I later read the detail, peculiar, not unnaturally, to that part of the world. I thought I would show my teacher a variety of dishes from this book which whetted my own appetite.

While seemingly impressed, she had already prepared some recipes for my introduction to cooking: spaghetti carbonara, meatballs in tomato sauce also doubling as tasty beefburgers, chicken wrapped in bacon with vegetables and new potatoes, healthy chicken jalfrezi and butternut squash.

All in half a day! To be fair my teacher only had me to contend with. I found myself in a class of one.

Following a short preliminary chat it became evident that we were both interested in Mediterranean-style cooking, such as Spanish tapas.

Most *tapas* menus on the island will offer bread drizzled with olive oil, rubbed first with a peeled raw clove of garlic, followed by a ripe red tomato. This is called *pa amb oli*, yet another speciality of Majorca. Nowadays any type of bread is used and could well be toasted. My preference is to have this on a slice of *pan moreno,* the local unsalted brown loaf.

For this *tapa* the dilemma which confronts Majorcans is whether the bread should first be drizzled with olive oil and then rubbed with a tomato, or the other way round. Either way they will add salt and, often for breakfast, either cheese, ham or *sobrasada*, another Majorcan speciality which is similar to chorizo sausage made from black pigs packed full of paprika and cured naturally. Delicious when sliced off into chunks and put on the *pa amb oli*.

Like wine, there are many varieties of *sobrasada,* cured over different periods, many home made ones being pretty spicey.

My teacher therefore went off script as she knew I was a frequent visitor to Majorca. I was quietly both pleased and surprised that I managed to prepare and cook potato and pancetta a la Glyn, spaghetti carbonara, meatballs in tomato sauce and to-die-for beef burgers with aioli. I came away feeling much better than when I entered the school.

The preparation allowed my excellent teacher to demonstrate the art of chopping onions, garlic and peppers without adding human fingers to the mix, as well as identifying a great variety of herbs which we chopped together and introduced to the dishes.

Unfortunately this was not the kind of cooking Maggie had in mind for me! Switching to Mediterranean dishes had not been her intention but rather the preparation of traditional English recipes such as roast meat and vegetables. I think I lost Brownie points, but I enjoyed the course!

I now can't wait to return to the sun kissed island and demonstrate my newly acquired skills to Jordi and his *amigos*. Quietly, however, I can only imagine they will be singularly unimpressed, preferring to return to their own peculiar brand of local cuisine, prepared in their inimitable Majorcan style amidst unintelligible banter between themselves.

Some things simply do not change, especially in the Tramuntana mountains.

Epilogue

So now you have it. Quite a journey. A journey in the sense of travel, certainly, but only as a means to an end. An existential journey; how we change, become wiser perhaps through education; widen our personal comfort zone.

No-one has the right to, nor usually experiences, an easy passage through life. No journey is that straightforward in whichever sense of the word is intended. Obstacles get in the way, either from the outset or along the way. Challenges are thrown out at every corner, though these sometimes produce opportunities. But it is how such obstacles and challenges are faced up to which help mould the character we become.

How philosophical are the lyrics to the simple child's song *"Every Journey"* which I have reproduced at the front of this book? Do have another look at the words. It is an added advantage that the music behind the lyrics is haunting. I was certainly moved when this song with its simple melody was taught to me by my grandson Jack as we strove together to climb a particularly steep mountain track leading us back to base after visiting the rock with the hole, Sa Foradada.

It is an obvious truism that those disadvantaged in some way will have a steeper psychological mountain to climb than others. Sadly many will be discouraged from the outset. But if such obstacles are to be confronted and overcome, certain fundamentals would need to be in place at the outset to facilitate the process of change.

In my case I was privileged to have loving parents who must have decided at the outset when I was born that for them sacrifices were needed so as to encourage me to succeed. At least I had that in my favour. A big plus.

They adhered to their Victorian values and, as if to prove the point, they enjoyed a happy marriage of 66 years until father died just one day before his 88th birthday immediately before Christmas.

Thanks to a major diversion taking us much earlier than intended off the M1 motorway travelling north from Solihull we were late for his scheduled funeral in Sheffield. All traffic was at a standstill. Mobile phones came into their own at that point. From the car I was in constant touch with both the funeral director and the understanding vicar with a sense of humour who rescheduled dad's funeral to the last one that day.

We were sweating to even make that revised timing, knowing that we were only minutes away from being told that dad would have to be returned to the funeral director's place until a fresh date could be found in the New Year. The post-funeral "celebrations" - if that's the right word – planned to be held in a central Sheffield hotel were also re-scheduled. What was to have become lunch turned out to be supper, or tea as they say in Sheffield!

No doubt dad didn't mind, after all he was always a patient man. He'd somehow know I would get there.

Well we just made it by the skin of our teeth. Dad was probably relieved. Better to be late than never!

Clearly there will equally be those born into harsh backgrounds unsupported by nurturing parents. Another important pre-requisite would come into play here: sheer grit and a strong determination to succeed. In any given situation luck tends to play a big part. To some extent however, luck can be manipulated or at least made. By getting into a particular position is an example, thereby increasing the chance of something happening which in turn causes an auspicious change in direction or fortitude.

Education was fundamental to my own determination to succeed.

Whilst unhappy at school during my early years and indeed throughout my time in senior school I was a bit of a swot and did pretty well in all my tests and examinations. I knew I wanted to attend college or university. Thankfully this was where parental support kicked in. I had no clear idea as to what I wanted to become. In those days no-one at my schools took the trouble to take me aside and advise me after any critical examination of my strengths.

Then, my best subjects were English, Maths and French, passing these subjects at equivalent GCSE level a year earlier than most. I had neither personable skills nor personality. I had spent my life thus far cocooned, sheltered in every way as only an only child could be. I know my mother had a difficult birth and was sadly unable to have more children.

As no real effort was made to identify my own particular forte I began thinking about a qualification involving the use of mathematics. I was also good at art so thought about a career as a draughtsman in some engineering company.

My father had no influence and could not reasonably provide me with any meaningful direction. Fortuitously this fell to my uncle who introduced me to a chartered quantity surveyor he worked with in Sheffield Borough Council. I was taken to a careers convention at Sheffield Town Hall, met someone representing the Royal Institution of Chartered Surveyors, took loads of leaflets and ended up enrolling on a 3-year full time course at Sheffield College of Technology enabling me to study from home. Not ideal, but the cheapest option.

I was to switch courses within a fortnight in favour of the valuation course, or estate management as it became known. From thereon I never looked back. I had three of the best years of my life, both working hard and, thanks to the guys on my course who befriended me, playing hard. Pretty exhausting stuff.

The swinging 1960's kicked in. Inflation hadn't particularly been thought about, the economy was buoyant, the country was in pretty good shape and the population was largely considerate and respectful of its elders. In short, people were content.

In those heady days I may have counted train spotting as a hobby, but at least coal-fired train engines belching out thick black smoke into the atmosphere in the 1950's and 1960's evoked a real sense of speed and mysticism. The heart beat increased to danger level in sympathy with the sheer dynamism of the express train thundering along single-mindedly intent on reaching its destination.

Unlike today, where the engines are either diesel or electric powered and entirely devoid of character, except arguably the high speed "bullet" trains. To my mind they are the equivalent to watching paint dry. Or, stretching the imagination, were we to consider these modern engines as humans as opposed to mere objects, we might describe them as having had a charisma by-pass!

Why therefore do I notice an increasing army of anorak-clad "anoraks", sadly of my age or thereabouts, who can be seen loitering at the end of the platforms at Moor Street and other suburban stations I've noticed en route to Solihull. Notebooks and cameras in hand they clammer to identify the numbers on the side of these diesel trains, appearing to go ecstatic when they observe an engine for the first time.

Am I missing something here? I don't wish to be unkind, but I cannot for the life of me see what can possibly be so exciting as a soulless object devoid of any character whatsoever pulling into Moor Street station and warranting such antics! Nothing can remotely compare with the enigmatic steam trains lost in a by-gone era, never to return, except when reconditioned by volunteer enthusiasts and driven along limited tourist routes.

I suppose one could construe that my moving from Sheffield to Birmingham, one industrial city to another having many similar characteristics and within easy reach of each other, was a move designed to stay within my own comfort zone. Though in my defence I knew no-one in this city of a million people and had to start from the beginning. This was to take a great deal of willpower and major dedication.

The reader will have noticed my willingness to undertake much work in the voluntary sector. This is particularly satisfying. Happily most companies encourage both employers and employees alike to become involved in this way. It builds character, devolves responsibility and teaches leadership, engendering a desire to help others without reward, at least in the material sense and not least creates lasting friendships.

The RICS taught me much about codes of practice and professional ethics. We did not however receive any basic grounding in business; that was self-taught later, after gaining work experience. Again, this comes back to character. Certainly in the professional sector, but, I suspect, in most walks of life, we must without deviation pay heed to our conscience. To do what is right for others. To clients and customers. Even our suppliers. This I decided at the outset should be a given.

Success is relative. It can be measured in many different ways, not simply in the wage packet. There are differing degrees of success. Drive and ambition will largely dictate where this leads. Rather like a bus journey, there are stops along the way where one can alight. Health and happiness also play a huge part in this ambition and aid the decision as to when to alight.

I have also attempted to look at my journey through life in contrast to that of Jordi's lifestyle in Majorca.

In my case I had a reasonable education which led to relative success in business. I developed wide interests and enjoy some travel. Jordi had no education, at least academically and hardly ever leaves the island, his life revolving around his family and close friends. It would be an oxymoron to say we are similar in different ways. But it is true. Jordi leads a relatively simpler life, mine seemingly complex. I see advantage in both our styles of life. It's just that Jordi's journey is shorter.

Majorcans, at least in the part we now live, seem a largely contented lot, oblivious to mediocrity or meritocracy. Life tends to amble along in the slow lane. Epicurian contentment is certainly a quality which the likes of Jordi, Miguel and Bernardo exude in bucketfuls. Their characters blend in well in this rural environment.

To travel beyond their own shores is not on their agenda. Why would they want to, they would argue. Maybe only when there is family to see on the mainland. Most things they need are found in their villages, their own gardens or in the mountains. Nothing much changes in Valldemossa. Or Soller. Or even in bohemian Deià.

At this point of my journey I have a confession. Quite a few months have flown by since I enjoyed attending that cookery course in Oxfordshire. Sadly I have neither found the time nor the inclination to roll up my sleeves, get in the kitchen and start cooking.

Let me be clear, I honestly don't believe my interest in the culinary art to be merely ephemeral. I will someday start in earnest. In mitigation my wife, who happens to be my biggest critic, thinks I'm too messy to be let loose in her working environment. The flame still flickers, it simply needs re-kindling – one day.

That gives me an idea for my next Christmas present from Maggie. No, not another celebrity cookbook. I'd never get this past the boss. Even though I've just seen one at half price! Perhaps another cookery lesson. Maybe. Maggie would say with conditions attached. But one thing I do need - more tennis lessons.

As my wife's interest in horse riding has recently been re-kindled I booked a couple of days in North Devon where she could go hacking – my 2011 Christmas present to her; for me a sight for sore eyes seeing a granny on horseback. Inca gets to come along for the fun. And I get to bank quite a few Brownie points! I need them.

It is impossible to predict with any certainty where life's journey will end. Or when. In life, as in books, chapters are continually opening and closing.

Discovering Majorca through the back door was a pleasant and unexpected eye-opener.

As dotage moves inexorably closer we are already considering a move off the mountains, away from the multitude of steps, steep inclines and narrow winding roads. Those who've met Jordi might jokingly suggest he is already in his dotage and that he for one would be quite happy to retire gracefully from working for us, thus avoiding the daily need to climb the interminable number of steps up to our *casa* so as to attend to his various duties.

Were I to suggest his retirement I'm pretty sure he would thank me profusely. Not for him much longer I suspect this quota of daily exercise!

I would however miss the daily contact with those idiosyncratic Majorcans!

I feel a final word should be given to our grandkids, who else?

Back in 2009 we introduced them to the West End, seeing Oliver at the Theatre Royal. This Christmas Maggie and I received separately framed letters addressed to Gran and Gramps:

"You are off to see the Wizard....the wonderful Wizard of Oz!!!

At 2.30pm on the 31st December 2011 at the London Palladium.

With Daddy and Mummy and most importantly US!!!

Love Freya and Jack xxx"

The experience proved a fitting end to the year.

Freya continues to develop in her singing. She has turned 10 and has just been admitted as a full chorister to Solihull School Chapel. Who knows, could this be a burgeoning career into singing on stage in a West End theatre? Maybe after an appearance on X-Factor?

As for Jack, he is already looking forward to honing his skills this next summer stalking unsuspecting wild mountain goats in Majorca's Tramuntana mountains.

Jack, the intrepid hunter, recently tugged my arm following a game of table football which we play at our Solihull home in the winter and asked:

"Gramps, if you're still alive by next summer, can we come to Majorca with you?"

Much earlier I'd discovered that he'd asked his gran the very same question!

Like gran, I had no answer to that. As seen through the eyes of a little boy by now just turned eight, anyone over his parents' age clearly must seem positively ancient.

Particularly his grandparents!

I conclude this account when most of the northern hemisphere seems to be in self-inflicted meltdown, economically speaking. With Europe's travails hindering the UK's economic revival everyone is blaming each other; passing the buck. Bankers, governments and regulatory authorities are all contributors to the economic mess which prevails in the USA and throughout Europe.

But no-one forced us to borrow more or live on extended credit. We were simply encouraged. Too much money seemed to be washing around. Now, the debt mountain seems too high to climb.

So, in the thought-provoking words of the song which Jack taught me and which now seem ever more apposite:

"When the battle seems too tough to win
Just remember this, we must stay strong.

Don't give up, just give it time.
Don't give up, just give it time."

My thoughts are already turning to what new adventures may lay in waiting as I resume this journey with Maggie in the summer holidays to Majorca, bags in one hand, the grandkids in the other.

I can't wait.

"An Ode to Grandma"

Busy fingers all day long,
Knitting socks and singing songs;
Running here and running there,
Picking toys up everywhere.

I wash your clothes, i make your bed,
I even see the dogs are fed;
I clean and sew and bake you cakes,
I nurse you when your tummy aches.

And when my aching feet are worse,
I do not scream, or shout or curse;
When little fingers curl round mine,
I know that i am doing fine.

Getting on my feet once more,
I hear a knocking on the door;
Grandpa's been and done his chores,
Sweeping paths and painting doors.

Off i go into the kitchen,
Now, my aching back is itching;
Cats and dogs rub round my knees,
I'm sure that dratted dog's got fleas.

Busy-busy sew and mend,

But it's coming to an end;

Your parents fly from sunny spain,

And grandma can go home again.

Florence May Pitchford (1918-2010)

Biographical details

Photo by John Hipkiss

Glyn Pitchford was born in Sheffield, Yorkshire, working most of his professional life in Birmingham after qualifying as a Chartered Surveyor. He represented the business community, serving on the Birmingham, Coventry and Black Country City Region Board. Glyn has been leading on work on the former City Region Board in order for next generation broadband to be rolled out across Birmingham, the Black Country, Coventry, Solihull and Telford.

He is currently representing the RICS on the Business Voice West Midlands Council and is an RICS judge for the annual regional property awards. Glyn is a well known businessman in the West Midlands having been Senior Partner of James & Lister Lea before merging the practice with BK, Chairman of BRMB/Capital Gold

Radio, Chairman of Countrywide Homes and Chairman of environmental business, Envirotreat, amongst other former and current business positions.

In addition to serving on the City Region Board, Glyn was until recently active in a number of roles serving the community such as being a Council member of Aston University and serving on the University's Finance Committee. He is a vice-chairman of the Birmingham Civic Society and a practicing Chartered Surveyor Arbitrator running his own consultancy practice.

In 1968 he married Maggie, whom he met whilst at college in Sheffield. They live in Solihull in the West Midlands. Glyn spends as much of his time as business, voluntary and family commitments allow, in Majorca.

Lightning Source UK Ltd.
Milton Keynes UK
UKOW032234130412

190694UK00001B/4/P